PERfecting
Property Conversations

How to Conduct Initial Property
Negotiations With Confidence

Rob McPhun

Book production by Powerhouse Publications, 2019.
www.powerhousepublishing.com

Contents

ACKNOWLEDGEMENTS

Any project, idea or book needs input, support and guidance from others and being a supporter profile (www.teamdynamics.com) I personally find that support important to my success. This book is no different.

I would like to offer my thanks to the following people who have helped me over the years to achieve many goals and who support me in wanting to go on and achieve even greater success.

Simon Zutshi, the founder of the Property Mastermind Programme who gave me the specialist knowledge and created the supportive environment to realise my goals in property and stretch me in my professional life.

Andy Haynes, property coach, mentor and friend who has always been there to guide and support me.

Paul Avins, founder of TEAMDYNAMICS.com and a world-class coach whose prompts, guidance and support helped refine the PERfecting conversations model and gave me the push to believe what is possible. (Still a work in progress!)

Jill Bos, the best mother-in-law you could wish for, and a supportive proof-reader.

Barbara Pajak (www.burstofcode.com) for the illustrations.

The many individuals involved in Property Mastermind and the PIN (Property Investor Network) community who support, guide, challenge and encourage others.

And finally, the best joint venture partner a person could have on their side, my life partner Nicola – thank you for believing in me so strongly even when I doubt myself.

INTRODUCTION

If you want to be successful in creating your wealth from property you are going to be making huge decisions that could have lasting and life-changing consequences not only for you but also those around you.

In fact, making sure there is clear communication between you and those affected by your decisions is crucial to your success.

Those decisions could cost you tens of thousands, maybe hundreds of thousands or even millions of pounds in financial losses, failed business and personal relationships, not to mention the negative affect on your health.

Surely, you want to get these decisions right or at least reduce the risk of getting them wrong?

Every product or service requires that at some point in the transaction we deal with people. In the business of property that could be suppliers, contractors and tradespeople, vendors, mortgage brokers, investors, estate agents, letting agents, accountants, planners, consultants, local authority employees, tenants, solicitors, and the list goes on.

It doesn't matter what strategy you are using for building your portfolio or wealth. Whether it is rent-to-rent, purchase lease options, buy and hold, conversions of commercial to residential, new build, houses in multiple occupancy, co-living homes, serviced accommodation, joint venture partnerships, etc.

It all requires you to deal with other people. Period.

Those dealings require you to COMMUNICATE with them. You need to get your message across, make sure it has been understood and that you have received their message in the way it was intended, and everyone has a clear understanding of each other's needs.

Sounds simple – we communicate every day, don't we?

Well yes, we do – and how many times does it go wrong? I would suggest it is more often than we would like to think but, on most occasions, it does not have serious consequences. We have a little misunderstanding with someone, a bit of discussion gets the situation clarified or sorted and everyone moves on. No harm done.

This book and the model described in it will help you not only reduce that risk but help you create the types of conversations that will generate property leads as well as assisting you to convert them into productive outcomes for all parties involved.

Dale Carnegie is credited with saying, *'Remember when dealing with human beings, you are not dealing with creatures of logic but with creatures full of emotions.'*

Most of us like to think of ourselves as rational, logical, thinking individuals who are balanced in our transactions and communication with others. In fact, the reality is the opposite. The emotional side of our brain responds far quicker to stimulus (a comment or conversation) than our cognitive, logical side. We mostly then suppress our emotions in order to communicate and interact at a daily level.

Think about it for a moment. We know that we are all different and unique.

What makes us so unique? (And before we go any further let me state: "No, this isn't a self-help book telling us that we are all special and unique and let's all celebrate that uniqueness and achieve anything we want!")

By "unique", I mean that we have all experienced different things in our lives. We've had different friends, teachers, parents, relatives, cultural influences, schooling, work environment, and so on. These experiences and influences have then shaped our personal attitude, values, beliefs, standards, and outlook on life.

This makes us look at the world in a certain way and therefore affects how we communicate. Why? Because communication is the way that we convey our thoughts and feelings to others. And those thoughts and feelings are influenced by those experiences we have had.

How does this apply to property? Well, if you're dealing with people you need to make sure that you are speaking the same language – and I don't mean just their dialect or vernacular.

Do you share similar values, ethics, and standards?

Do you have total clarity around what you have agreed?

Are you, as the saying goes, "singing from the same hymn sheet?"

Have you determined what their true needs are and not the needs that you have assumed or thought you understood them to be?

A phrase often used in property networking meetings and seminars is 'make sure you conduct due diligence on potential investors and deals.' But what does 'due diligence' mean to you and what does it logistically entail? The due diligence and research I conduct may be totally different from your perception of what it means. This book helps unpack such phrases and gives you tips to improving your communication skills to make sure we all understand what such concepts mean.

So, if communication is so important why do we keep getting it wrong?

The truth is that like anything we do habitually we can become complacent, lazy and closed to new ways of thinking. Communication is a skill. And like all skills it needs honing, developing and continually challenging.

The model outlined in this book will help you to re-skill, improve your existing communication skills and practise them whilst building your property portfolio or increasing your wealth through property.

Why am I so certain that it can help you?

Over the last 30 years, I have been helping my coaches and mentees apply this model so that they could move forward with their issues by having challenging conversations with others with confidence and ease. They have approached, what for them would have been challenging conversations and meetings with self-assurance and a structured plan to achieve their aims.

Latterly, after successfully building my own portfolio of properties and becoming financially free, I have been helping others do the same through property coaching and mentoring. Although we work through deal structuring and property strategies, by far the most common area we end up working on is their ability to communicate and build important relationships for moving forward to achieve their long-term goals.

Imagine being able to speak to vendors, agents, contractors and potential investors with credibility, confidence, professionalism and a natural expertise.

Follow the tips and strategies outlined in this book, and by following the model, you will!

CHAPTER ONE

THE MODEL

Let's look at an overview of the model first and then throughout the rest of the book we can explore it in detail with practical case studies and tips on how to use it.

One of the main differences with my model compared with others regarding communication techniques is that it starts with a crucial phase before the conversation or meeting even takes place. Rather than just thinking about the conversation or even worse 'winging it' as we go along there is the Plan, Prepare and Practise phase. The full model is:

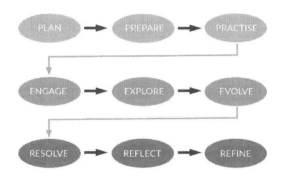

As you can see, it is a three-phase model and there are three stages in each phase.

What do they all mean? Well, I like to think that like most effective models it is simple, uncomplicated and easy to follow.

Using the model will not only increase your confidence, credibility and professionalism, there are many other benefits too. A great advantage of using the model is that by the end of the conversation you will have created an audit trail, used a structured and professional approach, and have a learning log for the future in order to improve for the next time.

Let's imagine that you have a conversation or meeting arranged with an investor, estate agent, or potential seller of a property. It doesn't matter who the conversation is with – the model covers all types of challenging discussions you may be facing.

And by "challenging", I mean challenging to you!

We all have different skill sets and personality types, so we all find different types of conversations and meetings challenging to varying degrees. Some people find it harder to speak on the phone than face to face or others are more comfortable connecting via the phone. Even if you are a person who has no concerns about walking into an estate agent's office with no prior introduction or meeting a potential investor for the first time, there is still something in the model for you.

Whatever your challenge is, this model is guaranteed to help! How can I be so sure? I have coached and mentored thousands of individuals in property, leadership, management, recruitment, promotion and personal issues over the last 30 years and all have benefited from using all or parts of the model to achieve the outcomes they wanted from meetings and conversations.

Going through the model, you will consider the first phase of Plan, Prepare and Practise for the meeting. This means so much more than just the logistics of time, date and location. Planning would cover, for example: what is a realistic outcome for the meeting and what do you want to achieve from that conversation? Too many individuals want to meet an estate agent, build rapport and trust, gain credibility, discuss properties and come out with a below market value deal which is the deal of the month – all within the first contact during a ten-minute meeting! No pressure then!

Why put so much pressure on yourself?

Having clearly defined, structured and realistic outcomes for the conversations gives you so much more confidence going into the session. By planning for the expected, and potentially the unexpected, you can relax more and free your head space in the conversation to focus fully on the issues that do come up.

You would then make any preparations necessary based on your planning, such as preparing your questions in writing, any comments you want to make, working on the questions or response you feel the other person might make and working through likely scenarios. Finally, there is the Practise stage. Depending on the subject matter of the meeting some are more challenging than others so might need more practise than others. Practise relates to possibly running mental rehearsals of those scenarios you anticipate, so you will be confident if or when they arise.

In the practise stage, you can run their potential emotional responses through mental rehearsal to a successful conclusion rather than a negative one. The practise stage might also include confidence-building strategies to help you feel less stressed before you hold the meeting.

But surely we all think about what we are going to say in meetings beforehand, don't we? That's nothing new.

It's good that you believe that you take the time to think about what you are going to say. However, I would suggest there is a vast difference between thinking about something and then implementing it properly.

Here's an analogy to help explain what I mean.

How many times have you gone into a supermarket to buy a couple of items only to come out with items you didn't intend buying? Oh, and forgetting what you went in there for in the first place because you became distracted?

I would suggest that the reason for this is because you have only THOUGHT about it and not planned it. If you had planned it by creating a shopping list and then applied that planning and preparation, you would stand a much better chance of getting your shopping right. It also saves time in the supermarket as you avoid the distractions of buying other products you do not need – not to mention the money you save!

Similarly, have you ever gone into a conversation knowing in your head what you wanted to discuss (your agenda) only to be distracted by their emotions, questions and issues (their agenda) instead? As a result, you realise afterwards you now need to arrange a second conversation to cover or clarify what you should have done in the first place. However, proper

Planning, Preparation and Practise eliminates this.

So, thinking about doing something and the actual planning of it are not the same thing.

By planning and preparing, you can stop worrying or stressing about what might happen in the conversation with the investor, agent or seller. This also helps you not to avoid issues you don't feel comfortable discussing such as financial background, ethics and values.

Rather than just thinking about the conversation and how it might go in our heads — which often leads to negative thoughts and 'what if' questions — with written planning and preparing and then practice added on, it means we can build our confidence, reduce our stress, and be more productive in the future.

Having a plan gets it out of our heads and frees up space to think more positively.

Moving on to the next phase of Engage, Explore and Evolve, that would be holding the conversation and what we and the other person do during this time.

The Engage stage relates to you building rapport with the other person, creating the right first impression and setting the tone for the conversation and making sure you are both ready to proceed. Building rapport and making a connection with the other person is vital to you forming the right relationship

I believe that, '*People will not buy from you until they buy in to you.*'

Your posture, language and tone are crucial to building your credibility as a professional, ethical, and trustworthy individual who they should do business with. You never get a second chance to make a first impression! Make it count in your favour. Undoing a poor first impression takes many more points of positive contact and effort — that's if it can be recovered at all.

I always think it is worth remembering that as you are forming an opinion about them in those first few minutes — and you know you are! — then they are forming one about you!!

As you progress from Engage to the Explore stage you will be asking appropriate questions, probing their answers and clarifying that you have understood what their issues or needs are. This is about probing in to the investors', agents' or sellers' needs and requirements and making sure you fully understand them, and they are sure of what you are proposing or can deliver.

It's important that if you want to create a win-win solution to their problem that you FULLY understand what their problem is!

Unfortunately, not all individuals you deal with will be completely forthcoming with their issues without some form of prompting or further delving.

This is where your range of questioning skills come in. You need to pose your questions but make it so it doesn't sound like a formal interview, and you do not sound robotic but remain genuine and natural throughout the process whilst still gathering information. We'll expand on all these things later as we go through the model in detail in later chapters.

As we explore their answers and the issues or needs from their point of view (their agenda) and then address our needs (our agenda), we can see that the issues that started the conversation may evolve either to a natural conclusion or into something different from the initial proposition that was originally presented to us.

I often ask my clients: "If a person tells you that they want to sell their house what is that they want to do?" They usually reply, "They want to sell their house." My response to that is you do not have enough information to make that judgement.

Think about it. The other person is making their decision to sell with limited knowledge of other property strategies. In effect, they do not know what they don't know. A rent-to-rent contract, purchase lease option deal, or exchange contract delayed completion (check your own country's property laws) may all be better outcomes for them once they are aware of them. YOU are the one bringing that specialist knowledge and expertise.

So, the conversation has evolved from initially what might have been a straightforward purchase to something that is far more suited to everyone's needs.

This is where you can start to use your specialist knowledge of other property strategies to formulate and create deals that are win-win rather than just making a deal that suits one party.

We then potentially move into the final phase of that particular conversation with the three stages of Resolve, Reflect and Refine.

The way we Resolve the conversation could be: agreeing that there is no synergy or agreement to be reached; deciding to meet again at an agreed date and time; or agreeing a deal committing to the clear actions that each party needs to take next. Again, as part of resolve, don't put pressure on yourself to come up with a definitive solution. Not all problems can be solved in one conversation especially if you are committing to long-term relationships, deliberating over deals of hundreds of thousands of pounds or making decisions that will have potentially life-changing consequences for individuals. Remember that an agreement to disagree is still a resolution at that stage. It does not preclude a follow-up conversation when appropriate.

Having concluded the conversation or meeting, we then move on to the final two stages of the model.

The real learning for you will come from the Reflect stage, and this again is so much more than just asking yourself, "How did that go?" and answering, "Ok, I think." Honest, balanced and objective self-reflection is a difficult skill to master and can take years to do properly. Often, individuals just do a quick examination of what occurred and think of the logistics and what the other person did or said in the conversation. True self-reflection looks at your part in the process in a critical way, analysing the good and the not-so-good. It's about being able to break down the conversation or meeting into sections or individual transactions. You might ask yourself for example:

Did I manage my emotions? How did I influence theirs?

Were my questions appropriate? Could I have phrased them better?

Were my answers appropriate to their issues? Was my response clear and credible?

Did I allow myself to get distracted or did I focus on the issues?

Self-reflection, whilst avoiding your own cognitive biases, is challenging and takes practice. Our cognitive biases are our values, beliefs, prejudices and current driving forces. Every thought we have goes through these cognitive filters so managing to think past them can be challenging.

One way to challenge our cognitive biases – and therefore help with honest, balanced and constructive reflection – is by using a coach or mentor. They should be independent, non-judgemental and help us to delve deeper into the processes that move us forward.

Having self-reflected or sought feedback, you can then think about what would be appropriate in order to refine your approach for the next time. What did you learn and what would you do differently? How would you change your questions, your introduction or your responses to their questions and issues?

The choice of what Refinements to make I suggest falls in to three main options:

1. keep the bits that worked the same for the next time;
2. change parts and test it in the future;
3. remove the parts that didn't work at all.

Again, bear in mind before refining we need to critically analyse why we thought portions worked, failed or were semi-productive.

Remember to be balanced and fair with yourself. Consider the parts that went well – congratulate yourself and maybe even celebrate your success. This re-enforces in your mind the positives for the future and helps build your confidence in the long term.

This is where the real power lies because as you refine and become more experienced your confidence grows, and you feel more comfortable addressing concerns that you might not have done in the past. You become more prepared to step outside of your comfort zone and stretch yourself.

Although the model is easy to follow, and it might make having a challenging conversation sound easy, the reality is you still have to focus and work at it.

Because you have a structured approach, you know where you are in the process and feel more comfortable because you have reduced your fear of the unknown.

Because it is SIMPLE does not mean it is SIMPLISTIC.

In fact, if you work through the model properly, because the conversations really matter to you, then it is still challenging. But I genuinely believe that it will make it far easier than trying to think on your feet, become distracted and unfocussed and it's that which makes all the difference.

Why not give yourself a better chance of achieving your goals for the conversation and getting the outcome that suits all the parties involved?

Now let's look at each stage of the model with loads of useful tips and strategies to help you achieve your goals and vision for the future.

PHASE ONE

CHAPTER TWO

PLAN

PLANNING IS DEFINITELY WORTH IT!

The plans that you make are sometimes proved wrong, but undertaking the planning process demands the thorough examination of all the options available. However, the knowledge you have gained during this examination is crucial to you selecting appropriate actions as future events take place.

All this planning, preparation and practise stuff. Doesn't it just seem like a lot of work to have what might be only be a quick five-minute conversation?

Let's run with the idea of only a quick five-minute conversation. How long does a transaction or interaction take between two people that could harm or even destroy a relationship?

Have you ever been in the situation where someone has introduced themselves to you at a networking meeting and you almost instantly made an unfavourable judgment about them? We don't like to admit it because it feels shallow, but studies show that we all often do it. Some research shows that we make assumptions about the other person in only a matter of seconds.

To be fair, I have been offended by someone just looking at me in the wrong way, never mind them saying the wrong thing. After that, it is always difficult to get the working relationship back to what it was.

So, if you are doing that with others, then you can safely assume that they are making those same judgements about YOU. Let's make them favourable and positive from the outset.

Because if the conversation is worth having, then, as it has been quoted, "Give me six hours to chop down a tree, I'll spend four hours sharpening the saw." Secondly, we can save more time overall by doing it right in the first place rather than having to have several more conversations afterwards to recover the situation or manage it fully. As we go through the model, we'll see that the whole process gets shorter with more experience.

The Oxford Dictionary defines a "plan" as, 'An intention or decision about what one is going to do. A detailed proposal for doing or achieving something.' I would suggest that before I decide to have the conversation, I would want all the information in order to make an informed decision about how that conversation should be conducted.

That's the concept behind planning and preparing. If you can reduce the perceived unknown aspects it increases your confidence, helps you sound more credible during the conversation, and it means you do not have to do so much thinking on your feet. What intrigues me is people spend more time planning for their holidays than they do dealing with some issues that could have a bearing on the rest of their lives. We get travel brochures, visit travel agents, ask friends and family for recommendations, read website customer reviews and then book for a fortnight's trip away. Often weeks and months of planning are involved.

Yet planning for a conversation about a deal that may cost hundreds of thousands of pounds, people just go straight in and try to 'wing it.'

Why risk it when you can plan it?

TIP 1: DON'T JUST THINK IT – INK IT

As stated in the description of the model, it is not enough to just think about the conversation coming up.

Write your thoughts down.

The mere process of writing down your plan helps the mind to focus, create neurological connections and gives you a record of your thoughts. It is also something you can refer to afterwards should you need to (see the Reflect stage later in the model) and helps you improve for future conversations and meetings.

Questions you think of, answers you might give – get them written down.

You can then work on them, re-write them as you hone them and get confident with the wording and their use.

Any ideas you have about brochures, due diligence on properties or people – note them down so you do not forget them.

Another advantage to writing your thoughts down is that they then prompt further ideas and concepts that follow on or spin off from the original thought. That way you can build a comprehensive catalogue of scenarios and planning ideas for the future.

TIP 2: GET THE LOGISTICS RIGHT

There are the logistics to consider, of course, such as setting a time and date to meet plus the right location.

What do you need to consider?

Ideally, you need somewhere private and confidential, where you are unlikely to be disturbed, with few distractions.

If meeting a potential investor, will the location reflect your credibility and professionalism?

Set aside enough time to feel focussed but not rushed.

How much warning should you give? How will you communicate if you (or they) are running late? This is all seemingly basic stuff, but is often overlooked or forgotten.

Getting the logistics right also satisfies those individuals who value timekeeping, attention to detail and being organised. These might not necessarily be high on your list of values but remember that communication is not just about you and you don't want to start off a conversation from a negative position.

If visiting estate agents and/or letting agents, how do you choose which ones to visit? It's not just about the geographical area you wish to invest in.

Are they part of a national chain or are they local independent agents? Who you choose to speak to will have a bearing on the type of meeting or conversation you are going to have.

Speaking to the owner and decision maker in the office is a different conversation from dealing with a member of the team staffing the reception.

TIP 3: SET A PURPOSE AND REALISTIC OUTCOME FOR THE CONVERSATION

Another aspect we need to consider is what is a realistic outcome for the meeting (the emphasis being on *realistic*).

Let me ask you a couple of rhetorical questions:

- Can you change a person's behaviour?
- Can you make someone do something they do not want to do?

We like to think we can, and I have seen many people try to do this with costly consequences. It is important to recognise that we cannot make anyone do anything they do not want to do.

Can we make an individual accept our offer or trust us?

No, we can't. They have choices.

What we can do is raise their awareness of the issues as we see them, the factors involved and communicate our understanding of the situation. By doing so, we can *influence* their choices, but we cannot make them do anything. I would suggest that just taking what I have said into consideration also reduces pressure on you managing the situation.

Why go into the meeting putting yourself under pressure, by trying to *make* them do something?

Be realistic about what you can achieve and do that to the best of your ability. Just remembering that will help you in the future to address issues with more confidence.

Often, when coaching, I ask the individual what they want from the meeting and their response indicates to me that they are putting too much pressure on themselves. For example, they state they are looking to meet an estate agent, introduce themselves, build rapport, create trust and come out with the deal of the year. All within the first conversation!

Yet when we break it down, they realise that a more realistic outcome for a first meeting would be a memorable introduction, clarity about what they're looking for, and an agreement to keep in touch in the future.

Similarly, when meeting an investor for the first time you are unlikely to leave the conversation with their bank details, a promise of future untold funds at your disposal and signed Heads of Terms in your pocket. If you did, I might question the wisdom of that investor!

I would suggest that often the conversation should be just an information-gathering exercise or a rapport and credibility-building meeting, or it may simply be to find out if there is any synergy between you. Based on that supposition some meetings or conversations may not last very long, and you will resolve to continue the conversation on another occasion. Building rapport and trust usually takes more than one conversation, so don't put pressure on yourself trying to achieve too much!

TIP 4: YOU CANNOT OVERPLAN

You may be concerned that you might spend too much time planning (and preparing). Don't be!

Yes, you may prepare for scenarios or questions that never arise in a particular conversation, but that doesn't mean they won't be useful in the future. Also, the fact that you have gone through the process of planning gives you confidence to address any other areas that come up that are similar to those planned.

As Benjamin Franklin famously said, 'By failing to prepare, you are preparing to fail.'

Going back to your potential concerns of over-planning for a short conversation (amount of time taken or becoming overwhelmed) – remember that as you become more practised and experienced, this stage gets quicker and easier to do.

In simple terms, ask yourself which of these feelings you would prefer:

feeling like you have over-planned and you've wasted some of your time or not having planned sufficiently and losing out on a great deal?

I think we both know the answer to that one!

TIP 5: PLAN FOR MULTIPLE SCENARIOS TO SUCCESS

Planning requires the thinking through of a variety of outcomes or ways in which interaction may take place so that you are not caught unawares in the actual conversation.

Based on your experience, and the knowledge you have gained from your due diligence, what are the likely scenarios that could occur?

- Is the vendor upset? (A probate sale? A divorce forcing a sale? Redundancy forcing the sale?)
- Is the vendor disinterested? (Retirement sale and downsizing with no urgency?)
- Is the vendor angry? (Divorce again!!)
- Is the vendor cagey and guarded? (A retiring landlord who has been in the business for years and knows the ropes!)

I am not suggesting you can predict the future, but by planning for several likely scenarios, you can build your confidence for any eventuality.

Another way to practise is to mentally rehearse potential scenarios that may occur in the meeting but, crucially, to run them through to a SUCCESSFUL conclusion.

When you *worry* about an upcoming challenging conversation, that is what you are doing – running a mental rehearsal, but unfortunately, leaving it unresolved or unsuccessful in your mind which naturally causes stress.

Next time you are thinking about what might happen, don't leave it unresolved. Work it through by planning in your mind to a successful conclusion.

TIP 6: PUT YOURSELF IN THEIR POSITION

Following on from the concepts above, a couple of good questions that I always ask myself while planning are, "If I was in their position, what would

I be feeling and thinking? and "What would I want from me (in this conversation) if I was in their position?"

Trying to gauge their interests or issues helps you to understand what is really driving them in relation to the decision they are making at this moment in time.

We tend to think that our view of the world is the only one (and sometimes the only right one!) and therefore we believe that everyone thinks or behaves like we do. This is not the case and it's where misunderstanding and miscommunication starts to take place.

Trying to think and feel like the other person is a great starting point for developing your plan for the conversation. Understanding their issue/position is crucial to formulating the types of questions they may ask you or the points that you might address in your answers. You may wish to consider questions such as:

Does the vendor need to sell, or do they believe that is their only option?

What does an estate agent want to hear?

What difficulties does a letting agent face each day that might impact their thought processes?

I accept that you are not a mind reader! However, by posing these questions in your mind during the planning process, it helps you to be more flexible in your approach and opens your awareness to other possibilities and strategies that you might not have thought of originally.

Don't pre-judge, but don't just focus on the obvious either.

TIP 7: BE SELF AWARE

So, when planning for any conversation, we must also consider our own values and beliefs and how they might affect our attitude and the behaviours we display to others. Bear in mind that it is useful to explore your own feelings around the perceived issue because, as we discussed earlier, it is very hard not to communicate your feelings through the tone of your voice, body language and the attitude you display.

Also, what type of personality are you? Are you a dynamic, fast-paced communicator or an intuitive people-focussed individual who sometimes talks too much and doesn't get to the point quickly? Knowing your personality type and how you communicate will help you to plan the changes that you need to make to accommodate the way others respond and communicate.

You can find out more at www.perfectingconversations.com and by taking the www.teamdynamics.com profiling tool.

Bear in mind your own Team Dynamics profile and that you may need to adapt to the selling profile of the vendor. Basically, although there are eight different profiles, they fall under four different energies who have preferred styles of communication:

Dynamo: visual, likes the bigger picture, fast talking; what's the best deal I can get?

Blaze: auditory, interested in relationships, social proof, talkative, likes stories; who have you worked with?

Tempo: kinaesthetic, based in the here and now, likes step-by-step plans, talks at a steady pace; when do I need to decide?

Steel: digital, logical, focused on numbers, detail, data and spreadsheets; how much and what is the detail?

Your planned conversation and questions should adopt the most appropriate style to *suit the other person* for what you are wanting to achieve, which may mean adapting your style slightly.

TIP 8: PLAN YOUR INRODUCTION

Let's think about your introduction or opening. This opening can set the tone for the conversation and demonstrate your credibility and professionalism.

Bear in mind that you may need different introductions for varying scenarios, but the core will basically stay the same.

You have control over the start of the conversation and therefore should use it wisely, productively and professionally. Lose control at the beginning and that is where you have problems and it becomes difficult to regain the initiative.

How many conversations have you had that went downhill right from the start because you failed to take control at the outset; where preparing a proper opening spiel would have made the whole process easier?

I know that by being confident and relaxed at the outset it has a positive impact on the other person; also, that my confidence comes from being sure about what I am going to say.

The skill here is to prepare an introduction that sounds professional and credible (but then practise it so that it becomes natural and conversational rather than a glib, insincere pre-set diatribe).

TIP 9: PLAN ON BUILDING YOUR CREDIBILITY

This is not only about building your credibility in respect of your property experience. It is about how you are going to demonstrate or highlight your life skills, life experiences and the qualities that you bring to the deal or relationship.

- How can you convey what your standards are?
- Do you have any examples of what your values and beliefs are in relation to conducting business and deals?
- What background have you got in deals?
- Have you got any examples or anecdotes that you are willing to share that demonstrate these standards and values?

Think about what recent deals you have concluded successfully and how you can convey them in a concise and structured way?

Don't be afraid at this stage to plan to share some of the challenges that you have faced, including deals that did not go according to your strategy. However, be prepared to demonstrate how you overcame the challenges and what you subsequently learned. So again, think about the examples you will use and how you can tell your story appropriately. This also has the benefit of preparing any potential vendor or joint venture partner for the reality that things do not always go smoothly and according to plan.

This is also a useful time in which to broach your thoughts on confidentiality, non-disclosure agreements, ethical practices and the idea that you use solicitors (where appropriate) to maintain legality. Think about: how can you do this and at what stage in the conversation?

If you haven't got these things sorted (for example, a financial broker, solicitor and builders – if required) then that is part of the planning. It sounds so much more professional if, when asked, you can answer with confidence that they are all in place.

This is about building your personal and professional credibility, including your reliability, your attention to detail, your working styles, your values and standards.

TIP 10: PLAN YOUR DUE DILIGENCE

A term that I often hear used amongst property investors is "Do your due diligence." Well, like the phrase, "Brexit means Brexit," the term is meaningless unless you describe what that due diligence consists of and looks like.

Plan your due diligence on both the property and the people you are dealing with. There has never been a better opportunity with the advent of social media and internet search engines to quickly perform background checks on locations and people.

On a property, check the various portals and property sales websites but also include others that I have highlighted in the useful guides in the addendums at the back of this book. (For the UK market).

In relation to a check on a person, list the sites you will conduct a name search on such as:

- Facebook
- LinkedIn
- Pinterest
- Instagram
- Google

In the Prepare stage, I have highlighted what you are looking for.

Also, list who you might contact to ask for their thoughts, experiences and opinion of the person you are going to meet or have a conversation with.

TIP 11: ASK YOURSELF, "WHAT DON'T I KNOW?"

Be honest with yourself about what you don't know – either in respect of your specialist property knowledge regarding strategies or building construction and works.

If an area is lacking or you feel a second opinion might be useful, then where can you get one?

At the time of writing this book, a popular strategy in the UK is turning single-family properties into houses of multiple occupancy to increase monthly cashflow. A great strategy – but do you fully understand the different requirements for planning and building regulations if works need doing and licensing. What difference will it make if it is in an Article 4 area? How do you check demand for rooms in the area you propose buying?

All this could affect your decision to either buy the property or otherwise use another acquisition strategy.

Can you accurately complete a schedule of works and then cost it? If not, how can you make a realistic offer for the property that means you have positive cashflow in the future?

TIP 12: DON'T GET PARALYSIS BY ANALYSIS!

There is a danger that with all this planning you start to persuade yourself that you don't have enough information, lack the specialist knowledge, or there are too many variables to think about. This could then lead you into paralysis and stop you doing anything. The best way to prevent this is to act.

You can take action by going in to the Prepare stage and getting ready to have the conversation.

CHAPTER THREE

PREPARE

The difference between the Plan and Prepare stages may be subtle, but it is an important distinction.

While planning to have a conversation can be more of a mental process, the Prepare stage means putting the "meat on the bones" by building on the structure and ideas that you have planned. For example, once you have your questions and responses written out, you may need to hone them by changing a few words or the order they come in.

There is a train of thought that suggests that if you compile a list of questions there is a danger you will sound robotic with the seller, estate agent, letting agent or potential investor. It is also suggested that you might be more concerned with asking your next questions rather than listening and responding appropriately to the answers coming back.

While these are valid concerns, and you should be aware that it might happen, you can make allowances for it.

Furthermore, I would rather you act by getting out there generating leads and deals – albeit sounding robotic and making a few mistakes – than not having the confidence to move at all through lack of planning and preparation.

The model allows for you to reflect and refine so you improve for next time. You will not improve if you don't get started to begin with!!

TIP 1: PREPARE YOUR INTRODUCTION

In the last chapter, we talked about planning your introduction, so you now need to sit and write it down.

Knowing what you are going to say at the outset – even for only a 90-

second opening – can also steady your nerves before you get into the full conversation.

Bear in mind that it should reflect you being honest and genuine in your property dealings and help set the tone for your relationship throughout this deal (and hopefully, if appropriate future dealings).

It should be natural, friendly and start to set you apart from other investors who approach agents, sellers and investors. It does not need to sound like a sales pitch.

How can you start to differentiate yourself from others who are working in the same area both geographically and strategy-wise as you?

You need to be memorable for the right reasons!

It does not have to be the same every time. If you are starting out on your property investment journey, then until you become completely relaxed and comfortable, I would recommend sticking with roughly the same content.

Be aware that if you are approaching agents, they get new investors coming in to their offices all the time – so why not help them to help you?

- What is your price range?
- What type of property are you seeking?
- Are you looking for yourself or other investors?
- Can you move quickly?
- Do you have cash?
- Are you looking to build a long-term mutually beneficial relationship?

Having an introduction starts to demonstrate that you are credible, professional and serious about moving forward.

If approaching a potential investor, a credible introduction starts to build the trust needed to create a fruitful partnership going forward whether it is on a fixed loan or full joint venture basis.

When preparing the introduction, be aware of how you could be sounding to the agent, vendor or investor and what their response might be.

If you have a foreign or strong regional accent, be aware that they might struggle to understand your first few words until they adjust their hearing to compensate. They will not hear any words you speak until they do adjust, so slow down slightly and think of them.

TIP 2: PREPARE YOUR LIST OF QUESTIONS

By writing out your questions, you will start to remember them; you can also start to sequence them so that they flow in a logical order.

List your questions about the property – (see Addendum) making sure there is a method to it. Possibly begin with the structure/fabric of the building first, working from the outside walls to the interior construction, from the roof to the ground floor, front to back, etc. Choose a method that suits you but also makes sense to someone else who you may send it to in the future if you are packaging up the deal and selling it on.

List your questions about the location and area – such as flooding issues, Local Authority Area Strategic Plans, transport links, major employers in the area, any planning restrictions (see Addendum).

List your questions about the person (see Addendum). Again, keep it methodical and then you will create patterns that your brain will find easier to remember. For example, "Do you have a mortgage?" If their answer is "yes," then there should be a series of follow-up questions such as: "How much is outstanding?" "Are there any arrears?" "What is the length of the mortgage and is it repayment or interest only?" "Have you any further borrowings against the house?"

Once you chunk up the questions in such a fashion, it makes it easier for you have a prompt word (such as "mortgage") that triggers the follow-up questions. Guard against sounding like you are interrogating the person, but a more natural style will come with practise.

As you prepare, the most appropriate language becomes more and more apparent and so you are not going to have to think on your feet. You can rephrase comments or sentences as you think of more appropriate words to make it sound more natural.

TIP 3: DEVELOP A PROPERTY CHECK SHEET

Develop your own version of a property checklist (see Addendum) using your own preferred style of recording information, including the use of technology/apps or good old-style paper. As outlined above, have a method for going from roof to ground floor, exterior to interior, front to back, describing the condition of each room, as well as potential works that need doing. Also, remember to take pictures with your phone (once you have asked and got permission to do so).

The check sheet is an invaluable tool for keeping track of each property you view, (remember: to generate great deals you should be doing plenty of viewings in your chosen area). This is both for your benefit and potentially for investors who you may pass the deal on to.

TIP 4: PREPARE A DUE DILIGENCE BROCHURE

How professional would it look if you had a pre-prepared brochure or file with your details, personal property background, expertise, professional values, ethics and methods of working?

Would it set you apart from most investors and property 'wannabes' out there?

It would demonstrate an attention to detail which helps to build your credibility, trustworthiness and professionalism.

I have coined a phrase, *"People won't buy from you until they have bought in to you."*

Communication is not just about the spoken word – it includes written material too. Some people like to handle material and have something to peruse later, rather than relying on verbal communication all the time.

It doesn't have to be glossy or expensive – modern printers can produce good-quality material relatively cheaply, although that is a judgement call for you depending on the level of investment you are at.

The file may include: your contact details, pictures and descriptions of works you have completed or deals you have secured, your credit rating, as well as your personal and professional experience.

TIP 5: WHAT ARE THEY LIKELY TO ASK YOU?

Imagine you are asking questions of someone and they start ermming and stumbling over their answers?

Would you be convinced they are trustworthy, professional and credible and want to do business with them?

So why put yourself in that position with a potential investor, seller or agent?

A major part of planning and preparation is anticipating the possible responses, answers or questions you may get from the other person. I am not suggesting here that you can predict the future. However, you can make some informed choices about planning and preparing for potential questions and responses.

How much more confident will you be if you have a toolbox full of your own responses based on their possible answers and questions? You're not having to scramble in your mind for answers, but you have well thought out and planned responses giving you credibility and assuredness.

List your answers to their potential queries (see Addendum) such as:

- How quickly can you complete on the deal?
- Do you have funds available?
- Do you already have a mortgage in principle?
- Have you completed this size of deal before?
- What property experience do you have?

The above preparation is even more important if you perceive you are lacking in experience, funds or knowledge.

Having a plausible answer prepared to cover a lack of property experience takes a significant amount of pressure off before you even make contact.

It is important to note here that you should not lie!

Be authentic, genuine and realistic in your answers.

An answer might be, "I am new to investing, but we all have to start somewhere don't we?" Pause and allow that comment to register in their minds and they will either respond positively or you can continue, "But I am keen to develop and be successful, so I have been educating myself (which you should be doing by reading, listening to podcasts, courses, being coached/mentored or just seeking advice from experienced investors) and I am looking to invest in property for the long term."

You should come up with your own wording to reflect the situation or circumstances you are at based on your property experience, so that it sounds credible, genuine and real.

Also, by writing your answer out, it starts to help you actually believe it – and once you believe it you naturally sound more confident.

TIP 6: DIARISE CALLS AND VISITS TO AGENTS

Being successful in any aspect of life, including investing in property, stems from taking ACTION. No amount of planning or preparation will help you succeed if you don't implement it.

Put in your diary the allotted times you will make calls to estate agents, letting agents and lead generators. You should consider making this a regular routine, so that you start to form good habits and behaviours.

Diarise the times and dates you will visit your selected area for investments and property viewings.

Go back to previous deals you have made offers on and follow up with the agents/sellers so see if the seller has become more motivated and needs to complete.

TIP 7: PRESENT YOURSELF PROFESSIONALLY

Ok, I get it. I should be allowed to be myself and people should take me as they find me. 'Don't judge a book by its cover' and all that.

However, if you want to present yourself as trustworthy, professional and credible then you need to look the part, sound the part and act the part! You may feel it reflects more on the person that you are dealing with that they prejudge you, but lots of research shows that people decide about our trustworthiness within a very short space of time (some research suggests merely seconds). Why risk making that judgement a negative one?

Prepare to wear the clothes that demonstrate your seriousness and professionalism.

I am not necessarily suggesting a suit and tie to speak to agents and sellers – although that may depend on your geographic area (Kensington and Chelsea) or property strategy (high-end conversions of offices to residential and dealing with commercial agents). There is no definitive answer to this, but I am saying give it serious consideration, think about the values of the person you are meeting and what they might be expecting and prepare accordingly.

Likewise, have quality, professionally-made business cards ready that help you stand out for the right reasons. Have you got a quality picture on your card? Is there a call to action for them to check out your credentials?

TIP 8: HAVE A POWER TEAM READY AND PREPARED

What do I mean by 'power team'?

If you're serious about building a sustainable, profitable property business that will run without you, then you are going to need a team of advisors working for you.

At a basic level, you will need an 'all-of-market' financial broker (not just a high street lender), an accountant who deals or specialises in property investments, and a good solicitor who understands creative property strategies.

An experienced builder and/or quantity surveyor (a person who calculates the amount of materials needed for building work, and how much they will cost) will also help with pricing possible building works and refurbishments so that you can calculate a realistic price for any deals.

In preparation, you need to put them on standby that you may need their services and diarise that accordingly.

In respect of the broker – have you furnished them with all your up-to-date details in order that all money-laundering checks (in the UK) can be conducted quickly and efficiently. I often speak to individuals who negotiate a deal that requires them to move very quickly, only to find that the broker needs copies of bank statements, proof of income, proof of residence, photo identification – the list seems endless when you need to move speedily! Be prepared and get it sorted beforehand.

In fact, once the basics are in place, you just need to update the records with the latest information and the financial broker may be able to give you a decision in principle very quickly.

Another benefit is that once the broker has all your details, then they can advise as to your potential borrowings which could affect your property acquisition strategy significantly. If they tell you that you are not able to get a mortgage or that you will need larger deposits than usual, this will help you to determine your strategy for acquiring control of property so that you can profit.

TIP 9: COLLATE ALL DESKTOP RESEARCH

Conduct and collate the desktop research you have on the person you are meeting and/or the property you are viewing. This will help you to remember the information you have gathered. Remember in Planning we stated you should conduct research on social media about the person. Make a few bullet-point notes about them so that it will be easier in the Engage stage to make a connection, build rapport and find common ground.

In relation to the property, collate comparables in respect of sales prices, rental demand and rent rates, as well as other details relevant to the area such as schools, transport links and employment opportunities. You may also consider research on schools, crime rates and anti-social behaviour reports. (See Addendum)

Once you have done this a couple of times for your selected investment area, the task becomes quicker and easier – like many of the stages of the model!

TIP 10: USE SOCIAL MEDIA FORUMS

Consider using social media forums to ask questions about an area, properties, letting agents or estate agents. Facebook can be very useful if you go into the right groups.

Use the search engine bar with keywords like rent-to-rent, or below market value properties and look through the list of hits. Select the larger, more active, groups to join and then ask away.

Be aware that the more specific your questions, the more constructive and useful the answers are likely to be – generic questions lead to generic answers! Lay out the circumstances fully of your situation and await the answers.

Make sure you also start to make an active and appropriate contribution to the threads, and you will start to find that people with deals and investors with money will actively seek you out.

Remember: naming and shaming is frowned upon as it is preferred that constructive thoughts and opinions are shared.

TIP 11: IDENTIFY YOUR KNOWLEDGE/EXPERIENCE GAPS

I sometimes hear new investors state that they 'don't do figures' or find it difficult to 'stack a deal' – often, despite them having undertaking property education seminars or courses.

I always remind them that if they think they cannot do something, then the chances are they will persuade themselves it is true – it becomes a self-fulfilling prophecy. Revisit this area of your knowledge and keep doing so until you become consciously competent. Indeed, once you get to know an area well, you will know the rent rate and therefore will know exactly up to what price you can afford to purchase for without pen, paper or calculator.

Also, what strategies are you in need of brushing up your knowledge on? Purchase lease options, rent-to-rent, freehold to leasehold, etc? Check out podcasts, books and other sources of property educational materials to help consolidate your knowledge and therefore your confidence.

Remember 'a little knowledge can be dangerous thing' and you are making potentially life-changing financial decisions.

CHAPTER FOUR

PRACTISE

There is a common phrase "practise makes perfect."

If you think about it, this is it not a helpful concept at all because we rarely become "perfect" at anything.

If we think we are perfect there is a danger we become complacent, or, if we keep striving for it then we are likely to be disappointed and stressed by our failure.

I much prefer the phrase "practise makes permanent."

Practise helps to create good habits and behaviours as well as helping us to build confidence, credibility and professionalism. We also become more natural in our dealings and unconsciously competent so that when something new comes along, we have the head space to deal with it.

Practise helps us to improve by highlighting our areas for development in an environment in which the consequences are less severe than if we make a mistake in a 'real world' situation.

You will still make mistakes in your dealings with others, but the place to learn from those is in the Reflect stage later in the model (which I shall come on to later).

Practise also helps us to turn the WHAT we should do into HOW we do it. From that HOW, even in the Practise stage, we then reflect and refine which creates our continuous personal and professional development.

TIP 1: VERBALISE YOUR INTRODUCTION

Get used to hearing your own voice verbalising your introduction. You will be amazed at how quickly your voice changes to a more confident and relaxed tone by saying the same words out loud several times.

It will help you to sound more natural as your confidence increases.

It also allows you to play with changing words, phrases and the tone that you use on key words to emphasise points.

Try saying it to a mirror at first. Does it feel awkward and silly? Of course, it does – but get used to it as all the best speakers, talkers and interviewers have done it!!

TIP 2: VERBALISE YOUR ANSWERS TO POTENTIAL QUESTIONS

This may sound even more awkward than verbalising a prepared introduction but it is definitely worth the effort of practising the answers to a few key questions you may be asked.

Again, it is the opportunity to listen to your own voice, changing words or phrases that sound unnatural or contrived into more appropriate and authentic answers.

There is no need to practise all the potential answers, but you should focus on those key ones that may impact on your credibility and experience.

Remember: do not lie, be authentic – but there are ways of sounding plausible whilst not revealing too much.

The above preparation is even more important if you perceive you are lacking in property experience, funds or specialist knowledge.

Having a prepared plausible answer for a lack of property experience takes a significant amount of pressure off you before you make initial or further contact.

TIP 3: GET CONFIDENT WITH FIGURES

To consolidate your learning and become confident with figures, then why not practise working out the return on investment (ROI) on potential deals before you attend a meeting.

Also, spend 10–15 minutes a day for several days doing dummy deal calculations, using pen and paper.

I realise that in this technological age we rely more and more on calculators and apps with formulas already embedded, so we don't have to do the hard, mental work. However, technology does sometimes let us down!

When I am delivering sessions helping people work out ROI, many are not able to do basic maths in their head or sometimes even just follow a set formula for working the figures out on paper.

Why is this?

I would suggest that it is because they have told themselves that, "Oh I don't do figures!"

Well, if they keep telling themselves that and reinforcing the message by not practising, then it becomes a self-fulfilling statement.

Get out of your comfort zone and practise.

It will build your credibility and confidence if you are able to assuredly state to a seller or estate agent that you have looked at the figures and inform them of what sort of deal works for you.

If you really feel uncomfortable with figures and maths, then find someone to work with who does understand them.

Be honest with the figures that you are using. Many investors either use over-cautious figures or over-generous ones.

Over-cautious figures are those that err too much on the downside of rents, voids, maintenance and bills costs. This will stop you doing deals that are potentially good investments. Analysis paralysis may set in and you will become frustrated.

Over-generous figures are those that factor in top-end rents, minimal voids, low or no maintenance, and too low bills. This may lead to making offers that are overpriced. Do not become a motivated buyer!

I recently sold a property and the buyer complained several months later that the bills they were paying were higher than they had anticipated – which we as sellers found strange because we had supplied them with all the previous 24 months' utility bill statements. So, even with the exact information, they failed to calculate the ROI properly.

Stick to the due diligence figures you researched and worked on in your Prepare stage.

TIP 4: USE YOUR COACH/MENTOR OR KNOWLEDGABLE FRIEND

If you have doubts about your introduction and answers or want to get your calculations checked, why not run them past your coach, mentor or other trustworthy person experienced in property and your specific strategy?

Have you not got one?

Then, the answer to that is simple – get one!! And quickly.

Many people think they can do it alone. Some are right, but most either fail to act through fear of getting it wrong or make expensive mistakes either in wasting time or money (or both).

Why risk losing tens of thousands in money when you can engage a coach or mentor who may only cost a fraction of the amount you are investing?

There are some who think that buying or acquiring a property is gaining an asset almost irrespective of where or what type of house it is. This is not helped by some popular TV programmes which very rarely place any emphasis on the downside.

Well, the wrong type of property, in the wrong area, purchased at the wrong price is not an asset – it is a liability and can cost you money.

I was at recent property networking event and whilst speaking to an 'investor' he told me about his purchases and was very proud of the fact that they were each only *losing* him £50 per month.

Yes, you read that right. Losing him £50 per month.

What was his rationale for those deals? He was going for capital growth – the long-term potential returns.

Ten minutes' coaching showed him the error of his ways!

TIP 5: USE ROLE PLAY

Being a trainer, coach, mentor and facilitator, I am a huge fan of using role play to check my learning, highlight potential issues and boost my confidence.

I realise that many people don't like to get out of their comfort zone and say that they find this form of practise 'unrealistic' or a 'false environment'.

However, after over 30 years of using the technique with clients, coachees and mentees I can assure you it is invaluable in highlighting both good and bad practice in your approach to people and the way you interact.

Practising a couple of role plays in a safe environment is one of the best ways to accelerate your learning, get immediate constructive feedback and develop quickly.

There is one big caveat here – use someone to role play with who will give you balanced, constructive and supportive feedback. Quality feedback can sometimes be difficult to hear (that's why honest judges on TV shows are not always the favourite ones but the most respected!) but it is also the most productive.

A further tip here is for that person to use a feedback model like 'Commend and Recommend'. In other words what did you do well and what would they recommend you do differently? This makes the person have to think of ways to improve your performance rather than just stating where they think you went wrong.

Remember: the role player should not create a no-win situation for you but be realistic and put themselves in the shoes of the seller, estate agent or potential investor. Conversely, they should not make it too easy either!!

The trick here is to create as realistic a scenario as you can with the emphasis on quality, balanced, supportive feedback.

TIP 6: VISUALISE – RUN MENTAL REHEARSALS

Many of us do mental rehearsals before an important meeting or conversation already – we just don't call them that.

I like to call them the "What if" rehearsals.

We get up tight and anxious because we start thinking about the conversation and then the little voice in our heads says, "What if...?" usually followed with a negative thought such as, 'I dry up and don't know what to say next,' or, 'they ask me about my experience in investing.' And that's where we usually stop thinking about it. Until the next "What if ...?" which starts to paralyse us from taking action.

What a pity that we run mental rehearsals only to a negative conclusion, when we could run them to a successful conclusion. They are only mental rehearsals after all. We can make them run how we want!!

Asking "What if...?" can be a debilitating question and doesn't always promote an answer.

I would suggest that changing your inner voices language to "What then...?" at the end of the question as it helps to promote a more positive, solution-focused answer.

Run the mental rehearsal and if you reach a point in the scenario where you feel an issue may arise, ask yourself, "What then...?"

So, as above: 'I dry up and don't know what to say. What then?' You can now plan for that scenario. For example, you could plan to summarise what has recently been covered in your conversation giving the appearance that you are clarifying things when you are giving yourself time to think of the next stage of the conversation.

Run the potential scenarios to a successful conclusion to boost your confidence, sound more professional and build your credibility in your own mind.

Also, running a variety of scenarios based on the due diligence (Planning and Preparation) you have done means that you will be thinking less during the conversation about the basics and therefore be able to actively listen more to the answers they give.

Whilst running your mental rehearsals also be aware in your visioning that you see and feel yourself entering into your conversation confident, bold and self-assured. Not arrogant or overconfident, but relaxed and feeling professionally competent. You make statements, ask questions or answer their queries confidently and credibly exuding experience and knowledge.

They are mental rehearsals after all – you can be the person you would like to be. This creates neurological pathways in your brain that will help you to be that person in the actual meeting.

TIP 7: MAKE CALLS AND VISITS OUT OF YOUR AREA

Another way to practise is to choose an area you are not thinking of investing in and do some viewings and visits to estate agents and letting agents there.

This may feel like you are wasting their time and it may also clash with some of your values – e.g. being authentic or honest.

However, would it not be authentic to state that you are looking on behalf of other investors? This could be true because although the area is not one you might invest in, should a great deal come along you could think about packaging it up and passing on the details to another investor who is interested in that location.

This is a great way to practise as it is, in effect, a 'live' situation but the pressure on you is not as intense because in your mind you are not necessarily getting a deal in that area. You will therefore feel less frustrated at any mistakes or issues that arise because you know the consequences are not so important.

Also, once you Reflect afterwards on your performance and highlight the bits that went well, you will boost your confidence considerably knowing you can do it for real!

There is no better practise than getting out there and speaking to individuals who are doing the work.

TIP 8: FEEL LIKE A PROPERTY INVESTOR

Another well-known phrase is, "Fake it until you make it."

This can be interpreted many ways and unfortunately for me it gets unwarranted bad press from some people because their perception is that it equates to being false or dishonest.

Even Richard Branson is credited with saying, "If an opportunity presents itself say, 'yes' and then work out how you can deliver."

My take on this phrase is: "If you want to be a property investor, then start thinking and behaving like one and then you can start delivering like one."

Basically, you believe what you tell yourself.

Tell yourself you are a property investor and start to think like one.

I'm not saying to make promises you can't keep, or mess people around with dishonest statements, but there are ways of presenting a persona that isn't false or inaccurate.

TIP 9: USE CONFIDENCE-BUILDING TECHNIQUES

If you feel that you need to really boost your confidence further, you can practise techniques both mentally and physically to empower you even more. These techniques are also useful in all areas of your life where you feel you would benefit from being more confident.

Although there is research indicating that our thoughts affect our behaviour and actions, there is more and more evidence to suggest that our physical actions, stance and bearing also impacts on our thoughts in both a negative and /or positive way. (See Amy Cuddy's book, *Presence: Bringing Your Boldest Self to Your Biggest Challenges.*)

Become aware of your posture in certain situations and practise walking tall, standing erect and being positive in your movements. When seated, sit up straight and slightly forward showing interest and alertness. Notice how positive that makes you feel compared with slouching, shrinking backwards and disinterested.

So, our actions and posture have as much bearing on our feelings as our thoughts – make them positive, assertive and deliberate.

There is also a technique from Neuro-Linguistic Programming (NLP – Richard Bandler and Dr John Grinder) called "anchoring" which can be used to trigger confidence when you need it most.

Setting an anchor is a 4-step process:

- **Become clear about the confident state you wish to be in** – e.g. bold, self-assured, assertive and dynamic.
- **Think of a time in the past when you have been in this state** – it does not have to have been in a similar set of circumstances – it's the *feeling* you are after.
- **Relive that experience as vividly and intensely as you can** – remember the sights, sounds, smells, and most importantly, the *physical* feelings (like a heightened awareness, positive posture) and *internal* feelings (such as pride and accomplishment).
- **Now create an anchor to trigger the same feeling in the future** – this anchor is usually a hand movement, albeit one you do not normally make, such as gripping your thumb and little finger together firmly for a few seconds and then releasing them. This makes it a deliberate act that you can use in the future and creates a pattern in your brain which triggers the feeling.

Some people find that repeating steps 1 to 4 several times helps to create a stronger anchor.

You can then use this anchor just prior to going into a meeting or walking into an estate agent's office or meeting a seller.

Little rituals or clothing can also become anchors – watch sports people who use them all the time. Nadal's serving ritual in tennis is a classic!

PHASE TWO

REAL ESTATE
AGENT

CHAPTER FIVE

ENGAGE

So, you've gone through the first phase of the model in Planning, Preparing and Practising – it's now time to take action and move in to the second phase of the model which is Engage, Explore and Evolve.

Let's put that hard work into tangible actions that keep you moving on your journey into property investment.

It is often said that "you never get a second chance to make a first impression," and whether we like it or not it's true.

I find it quite fascinating that we are guilty of making quick judgements about people based on the flimsiest of criteria, yet we don't expect people to do the same about us.

I know some people will be reading this and thinking, 'I don't' or 'Don't include me in such a sweeping statement,' but research backs up exactly what I am suggesting.

Dr. Travis Bradberry is co-author of the bestselling book *Emotional Intelligence 2.0*. He says that psychologists at Harvard Business School found that we make snap judgments about other people that answer two primary questions.

Subconsciously, you and the people you meet are asking yourselves:

"Can I trust that this person has good intentions toward me?" and

"Is this person capable?"

So, even if you don't feel it is right how you think about others, it will be probably be right about how they think about you so why risk creating the wrong impression with them.

Use the following tips for going into the conversation with a seller of a property, or an estate agent, a letting agent or a potential investor.

TIP 1: FIRST IMPRESSIONS COUNT

Following on from the above, you will hopefully be wearing appropriate clothing for the meeting based on your due diligence on the person or type of meeting. I would go as far as to say even consider your means of transport to meetings and where you park it – possibly out of view or choose another mode. I once turned up to a house viewing in a socially-deprived housing area and another potential viewing buyer parked outside the house in their Bentley motor car. It was probably worth more than the whole street! That Bentley owner was not considering the possible effect driving such a car would have on the seller. It could be admiration, but it could just as easily be envy, jealousy or resentment. The seller did not do a deal with the Bentley owner that day!

Ok, you can argue that it might say something about the seller's values but at the end of the day you're there to build a relationship with the other person, negotiate with them and eventually get a deal.

I am not saying don't be yourself, but also consider the likely expectations of the other person you are dealing with.

People do business with people who they know, trust and eventually like.

Remember my phrase: *'people won't buy from you until they buy in to you,'* which means developing the trust and credibility that they then want to do business with you.

Dressing the part can also be used to boost your confidence – in effect, you are wearing a uniform that creates a neurological feeling of, 'I'm a property investor/developer/owner.'

I generally wear the same shoes, which have become my confidence anchor.

During your practise phase, you got used to using your body presence to create a great impression, so now is the time to apply it.

Walk in standing tall and upright, looking positive and purposeful. The trick is not to be overbearing or dominant, but appear confident and relaxed.

By the way, we stated in planning and preparation that you should get the logistics right in respect of the time of the meeting/conversation.

Your first impression with many people will also include turning up on time so that you are not be flustered or panicky because you are late.

You may have even considered sending a message that you had set off and were on your way – updating them if you had got delayed along the route.

Little things matter especially to different personality types!

TIP 2: BUILD RAPPORT QUICKLY

Following on from making your approach, you now need to build rapport and trust as quickly as you can. Irrespective of the type of meeting, there are some common themes to building rapport.

Introduce yourself by your name and make sure it is clear and understood. If you have a strong foreign or regional accent, consider that the other person will initially have to strain to listen and pick up on what you are saying.

This may seem a minor thing but, believe me, if the other person is having to work too hard to hear you, then they will soon 'tune out' and miss important details. (See active listening tip).

Do you have an unusual name? If so, again consider the other person and make it easier for them to understand. I have spent my whole life saying my surname slowly and deliberately because people never believe its pronunciation on first hearing. I am understanding and tolerant about it because communication is about getting your message across – not sticking to personal principles! In fact, it often breaks the ice and adds a bit of humour. Could you make use of yours in a similar way?

Smile as you start to speak and keep good eye contact. If appropriate, shake hands being aware of cultural differences and respecting other people's personal space.

Is there a science to shaking hands? I am not a massive advocate of the nuances of the different types of handshakes, but I think it is sufficient to say it should be a genuine shake of the hands – not too limp or half hearted and certainly not a power struggle of who has the firmest grip!

Listen for their name and remember it! Use it several times early in the discussion as this serves to help you remember it and confirms to them that you heard it and are interested enough in them to use it.

I know you have practised an introduction and now is the time to consider which part of it you should use, if at all. Having practised it means it will have given you confidence should it be needed and now you can make a judgement call as to whether the time is right. If not, go with the flow of the conversation.

TIP 3: FIND COMMON GROUND

As a general rule, we all like people who are like us.

During this initial conversation, you are listening for something that you both have in common.

Based on your earlier due diligence, you may be aware that they have a similar taste to you in sports, music, hobbies or interests. You can introduce this by saying something like, "I see from Facebook that you follow Grimsby Town football club...I also..." or whatever the link might be.

This demonstrates that you have taken the time to get to know them before you have even met them showing interest, professionalism and attention to detail.

People call it small talk, but it is actually very important in helping to build rapport quickly and establishing a connection. We like to connect with people.

If you are at a seller's house for example, you may see pictures or ornaments from around the world which may be places you have also visited. If so, comment on them and show interest. Don't overdo it – you are there to negotiate a win-win deal – but they are more likely to deal with someone they can also relate to. It isn't always about price.

If the conversation is with estate agents, then the small talk may be about how property is performing in the current market, what new legislation is coming in and how it might affect them – get them talking about what might interest them.

If meeting a potential investor – the rapport building is the same only the comments might be about their interest in property, the length of time they have been in property and what they think the future looks like for property investments.

People like giving their opinions.

A word of warning here though. Small talk should be about them, making a connection and building trust. Stay away from controversial, emotive or divisive topics. Even if they proffer a view that you disagree with, do not get drawn – remain neutral at this stage unless you feel a real connection and then you may consider offering your thoughts.

This generalised talk is also useful for you to start to get a feeling for their personality type – and you can then start to respond to them in the most effective way.

TIP 4: DEVELOP YOUR ACTIVE LISTENING SKILLS

It's a phrase that is used a lot but active listening, like many things, is a specific skill that needs to be developed, practised and then honed.

One of the reasons we sometimes lose interest in what a person is saying is because our brains can process about 400 words per minute whereas the person talking to us speaks at a rate of about 120-150 words per minute. This means our brains work faster than they can speak and we like to fill in the gaps!!

You should master this skill and it will serve you well in many aspects of your life.

Learn to ask a question, stay silent, stop your mind wandering and then just listen to the other person's reply. Don't start forming an answer to their reply or filling in the rest of the sentence before they finish.

Also, pay attention to the non-verbal cues that you can pick up on because you are not focusing on just the words and forming your reply. This becomes even more important in the Explore phase but for now, let's focus on just making that connection to build rapport.

Reduce things that may distract you such as mobile phone notifications, being in a busy area, and background noise.

Do not be too quick to fill a pause in their speech and be patient – letting them finish their sentence. Do not finish their sentences for them! Some people take longer to formulate what they want to say, so roll with it.

We can recognise a great deal of information about each other without saying a word.

When you are face to face with a person, you can feel their enthusiasm, boredom, or irritation very quickly in their expression, the set of their mouth, the slope of their shoulders. These are clues you shouldn't ignore. When listening, remember that words convey only a fraction of the message and you should learn to read the intent behind the words or make sure you clarify your understanding of the message.

In the workplace, I used to call this the "cup of coffee comment." A team member might ask if I wanted to go for a cup of coffee. I often knew that this really meant, "I'd like to have a chat with you about something important, or personal or confidential" and once we were chatting over the coffee, they would eventually get round to telling me the real reason behind their invitation.

During this Engage stage, you should be looking for those cues that indicate to you what the real reason might be for the vendor selling the property, or what the investor is looking for in any arrangements, what is important to them and their values and ethics.

What is driving the estate agent and their agenda?

In our local area we knew that HMOs (House of Multiple Occupation – shared living accommodation) had a very poor reputation with a history of police raids, drug abuse and anti-social behaviour by the tenants. Being local estate agents and living in the area themselves, we knew they were also reluctant to sell houses to be turned into more HMOs.

How did we overcome this?

We connected with them by explaining our background of being ex-police officers, we were aware of the issues and we went on to fully explain how ours would be different, up-market, quality homes which would be actively managed, and issues would be dealt with swiftly and appropriately.

The result? We allayed their concerns first before we even talked about deals for houses. We got a call regarding an off-market house that suited our needs perfectly two days later. A win-win situation.

Actively listening to the other person's values, concerns, issues and real agenda means being open-minded, not becoming solution-focussed too early in the conversation and picking up on the things not verbalised.

TIP 5: CONTROLLING EMOTIONS

If you are picking up on the emotions and nonverbal cues of others, then guess what?

They are also picking up on yours.

I am not saying be a poker player or to be like Data, Spock or some other non-life form Android robot! Be natural and authentic or they will see through you.

It is difficult though not to show your disapproval when you walk into someone's house and it is in an appalling state with muck and filth everywhere and smells disgustingly of animal waste. If they live like that, then it is normal to them, but they will pick up on your discomfort if you show it in your face or comments. (Extra tip here – when you know it is going to smell badly, smear a thin layer of strong-smelling Vicks nasal decongestant under your nose to hide the other odours. I used this in the police and you can imagine some of the situations and premises we went in needing something to counter the smell!)

Another scenario when you may show your emotion is when you ask about the price they are expecting for the sale of the house, and you know it is unrealistically high based on your research.

Similarly, it is hard not to show over-eagerness if they have priced it right and it matches all your criteria for a good purchase.

How do you manage your emotions in the heat of the moment?

- Be well-prepared – if you have run the scenario through your mental rehearsal, then you will have planned your responses.
- If necessary, take a short break from the conversation so you get time to recoup your thoughts and become more logical.
- Breathe deeply a couple of times (unless in the smelly house!) and mentally count to five.
- Like anchoring a feeling of confidence, you can anchor a feeling of calmness – now is the time to trigger it.
- Ask questions unrelated to the area that is emotional and then, when you are more logical, return to the topic.

What about if the other person becomes emotional – bearing in mind that the reason for the house sale could be due to circumstances such as divorce, redundancy or bereavement in the family? Again, this is something that hopefully you uncovered in your due diligence during the preparation stage.

How do you influence their emotions?

- Be prepared – from your due diligence on the sale of the house, could you have expected this and planned accordingly?
- Have tissues ready in your pocket. You probably won't need them, but offering them shows support and understanding.
- Show empathy by allowing them the time to dissipate their emotions.
- Be prepared to postpone the meeting, if necessary.
- Do not try to tell them you understand their position or feelings – you don't – as we all respond differently to similar stimuli.

It is unlikely that an estate agent or potential investor would become emotional, although if the investor had a previously poor experience with a scheme or individual, then who knows?

It is always worth remembering that when dealing with people, you very rarely know their back story or full background, so although you can't be prepared for every eventuality, pick up on those emotional cues and expect the unexpected.

TIP 6: SPEAK PLAIN LANGUAGE

Avoid using property jargon unless you are dealing with another investor or property professional and even then, only after you have clarified their understanding and level of knowledge.

Besides creating the possibility of confusion, it can make you sound like you are trying to impress a little too much with your knowledge, which is not helpful.

It's amazing how different professions and industries have their own terminology for things, as well as scores of acronyms or definitions.

So, make sure you put what you want to convey as your message into ordinary language.

We often talk about offering the seller 'speed and certainty' of sale. Is that how you would say it – "I can offer you speed and certainty of sale" – or might it be more appropriate to say "I have the funds available and my broker and solicitor can be ready to move as soon as we agree a deal"?

Avoid acronyms and their strategy titles like PLO (purchase lease option), rent-to-rent, EDC (exchange contract, delayed completion), DIP (decision in principle). Keep it simple and, without being patronising, explain it as if they are new to property.

I have experienced it where I have been explaining the concept of a purchase lease option to a seller and they have replied, "Oh, you mean like a PLO." It turns out they had some knowledge of property acquisition strategies and the conversation moved on quickly from there.

TIP 7: BE AWARE OF CULTURAL DIFFERENCES

When dealing with other people, we need to bear in mind their values, beliefs and cultural backgrounds and treat them accordingly.

Show respect when speaking and interacting with individuals. Here are some things to be aware of:

- Eye contact – whilst we should maintain eye contact to show interest, be aware that some cultures avert their eyes more (Asian and Arabic) whilst others regard eye contact as important (Afro Caribbean). In fact, they can sometimes make you feel intimidated without their knowing it.

- Touch – some cultures frown upon touch between sexes, including what in the West, we perceive as "normal" (eg. shaking hands or placing a hand on a shoulder).
- Personal space – again, in the West we are more inclined to be protective of our personal space, whereas Asian cultures are less protective.

The intention is not to stereotype individuals but to raise your awareness of what may be going on during the early stages of your conversation so that you do not accidently offend or become offended by the other person.

TIP 8: REMEMBER TO ASSESS THEIR PERSONALITY TYPE

During this stage you should be asking questions to find common ground, build rapport, actively listening to the answers and based on their responses making an assessment as to their personality type.

Bear in mind your own Team Dynamics (www.teamdynamics.com) profile and that you may need to adapt to the selling/buying profile of the vendor. Basically, there are four different energies and they respond differently in their communication styles;

Dynamo; visual, likes the bigger picture, fast talking, likes bullet points, what's the best deal I can get?...

Supporter; interested in relationships, social proof, talkative, likes stories, who have you worked with?

Tempo; based in the here and now, like step by step plans, talk at a steady pace, when do I need to decide?

Steel; focus on numbers, detail, data and spreadsheets, how much and what is the detail?

Listening to their answers you should adopt the most appropriate style to *suit the other person* for what you are wanting to achieve which may mean adapting your style slightly.

TIP 9: BE PREPARED TO WALK AWAY

Even in the early stages of a conversation and forming a relationship, be prepared to walk away, albeit in an appropriate and professional manner.

If speaking with a vendor, be ready to walk away if you get the feeling they are not motivated enough to sell or may be more trouble to negotiate with than the deal is worth. Life is too short and, if you have a good lead generation system in place, there are always other deals to be had.

It takes an enormous amount of pressure off you if know you do not have to do a deal.

Your time and energy are limited – use them wisely.

If engaging with a potential investor, your initial face-to-face meeting is to find common ground between you, understand their needs, establish their values, ethics and standards making sure they complement yours. If they don't match or you feel there will be dysfunctional friction, be prepared to exit. This can be done with the understanding that you will keep their details, and should something come up with you (or someone else you know), then you will re-contact them in the future.

Saying "no" now saves doing it later and before any harm or financial losses are suffered.

CHAPTER SIX

EXPLORE

Of the hundreds of people I have coached over the years, an area that we often discuss the most is this Explore stage following their meeting or conversation with a seller, estate agent or potential investor. It usually revolves around their lack of questioning, or poor questioning technique, or lack of clarification of the information they have gathered during a conversation or meeting.

They have often come away with too little information because they did not want to ask the perceived difficult or embarrassing questions.

You cannot resolve an issue unless you truly understand what the issue is.

This means exploring the true needs, wants and concerns of the seller or potential investor. They are not always ready to share this information with you until you have established trust and rapport as highlighted in the Engage stage.

You cannot create a win–win situation unless you know what a win looks like to them!

TIP 1: THE A.B.C. OF EXPLORE

Without wishing to sound too cynical or mistrusting of people, there is a general set of principles that you should consider applying in your dealings within business (and important areas of your life too):

- Assume nothing,
- Believe no-one,
- Check everything.

Now, how far you take these sentiments and apply them is up to you, but if you bear them in mind during your conversations and meetings, you will be more productive and successful in your outcomes.

You should not make it seem like a police investigation or inquisition. Once you become skilled, you can make it sound like your questioning is showing deep interest and concern for their needs and resolving their issues.

TIP 2: FOLLOW A NATURAL, CONVERSATIONAL PATH

By now, having done such an excellent job in building rapport and trust during the Engage stage you are in a natural free-flowing conversation and you can move into the reasons for the meeting.

Allow the conversation to move along naturally and pick up on their responses with you own appropriate replies, follow-up questions or comments. This is where you start to hone your listening skills and can reflect on your responses later after the meeting.

Remember that because you have planned and prepared the areas and topics YOU wish to cover, it allows you the flexibility to go with the flow but then return at an appropriate time back to those areas.

This is also where one of the strengths of having the PER structure becomes apparent too – when it stops you becoming distracted or diverted from the issues by the other person.

Again, be aware of different personality types who will have a different conversational style. If you are a Blaze energy, you will find talking and story-telling perfectly natural, whereas a Steel energy person may come across to you as having a cold, blunt almost offensive, style of talking. The Steel person will want you to get to the point quickly.

There are also cultural differences in conversational style in that many Eastern European cultures have a matter-of-fact, straight-talking manner that Western cultures can interpret as mildly aggressive rather than their intention of being honest, professional and efficient.

To maintain that trust and rapport, adapt your style to match theirs without compromising your standards and approach.

TIP 3: SILENCE IS GOLDEN

I believe that one of the most powerful strategies you can use to get people to open up and reveal more is through the appropriate use of silence.

Generally, we hate silence, so it usually gets filled by someone.

Try it when you are next in a conversation. Rather than immediately respond, wait a few seconds (and that's all it takes – a few seconds), and the other person will then fill the void with something else they want to say.

If you are in control and are managing the conversation, then you can ensure that the person filling that silence is them. This will lead to them expanding on what they have just said and often results in them giving more information away than they intended.

Remember, if you are speaking, they are not. You only learn something new when someone else is speaking!

The other advantage of using silence is that it does make sure that they have finished articulating what they want to say before you reply.

Like all useful techniques, do not overuse it as it loses its power and starts to become unnatural.

I once worked with a colleague who became known as 'The Ice Man' due to his overuse of silence. It made some conversations with him eerie and a tad intimidating!

TIP 4: TAKE NOTE OF TONE, BODY LANGUAGE AND KEYWORDS

It's important during Explore to pick up on their emotional cues, body language and tone of voice (as we looked at in the Active Listening tip).

Keep monitoring their posture and gestures to see if they become agitated, uncomfortable or distracted. Again, don't turn it in to an interrogation, but gently prompt their responses with follow-up questions to make sure you are understanding what is going on and what the real issues are.

However, it is also useful to listen for keywords or throw-away phrases that are added on almost as an afterthought. These sometimes indicate there is more information behind the answer.

Watch out for add-ons to a sentence like:

"…not at the moment."

"…not really."

"…etc."

"…as everyone knows."

I would be considering asking them to clarify those add-ons with follow-up questions.

TIP 5: CLARIFICATION QUESTIONING TECHNIQUE

There is a simple model for applying the A.B.C of the Explore stage which is:

Area – Probe – Clarify – Summarise

This means:

Area – talk about the area of interest.

Probe – their responses with your questions for further information.

Clarify – that your understanding of those answers matches their intended message.

Summarise – back to the person what they have said – and move on to the next area.

I am not suggesting that you apply this at each stage of the conversation, but again it is a useful tool for you to use at various points especially around key areas.

As an example, you might ask: "Do you have a mortgage outstanding on the property?" and the seller replies that they do. Your follow-up questions might be:

- How long is left on the mortgage?
- What type of mortgage is it?
- What are the monthly payments?
- Is it a fixed rate or variable?

- Is there a penalty on redemption?
- Are you up to date with payments?
- Whose name is the mortgage in?

Once you have probed and clarified that, you can summarise the information and then move on to the next area of interest.

You may be thinking as you read the above that to ask all those questions will start to sound like an interview, but that is where your skill comes in of making it all sound like part of the conversation.

Worried that you will sound like a police investigator? At first, it may sound a bit stilted and false, but you have to start somewhere.

Maybe lighten the mood, if needed, by adding a joke such as, "Blimey – sounds like I'm giving you the third degree!" and you can follow this with "I realise I'm asking a lot of questions but, in order to fully understand how I can help you, it's important I get all the information to make a decision that suits us both."

By doing that, you are turning the situation around into a way of helping them and that's what you are there for.

TIP 6: TYPES OF QUESTIONS TO AVOID

You may have heard of the 5WH Questions – Why, What, Where, When, Who and How. Other than the overuse of the 'Why' question, they are all staples of a good, open-question technique for eliciting information from individuals during a conversation.

The word of warning over using 'Why' question is that it can (under some circumstances) come across as challenging to the person being spoken to.

Think back to when you were a child (or if you have children yourself) your/their constant use of the why question often ends in frustration and being told, "Because I said so! That's why!"

Rather than asking "Why?" you can use, "What makes you ask that?" or "Can you expand on your thinking behind that?" for example.

Avoid using multiple questions (where you string several questions in to one sentence). It can become confusing as the person does not know which question to answer first and you also don't know which they have answered!

Use closed questions when necessary to check out understanding and to clarify what they have said. This is especially useful when you feel you have collected all the information and you are reaching the point when a decision to resolve the issue needs to be made.

Beware of using leading questions – these are generally where you have assumed a detail or fact and have asked your question based on that assumption. We particularly use these when we think we understand a situation.

In the example above regarding the mortgage, early in my property journey I made the mistake of assuming that because someone had lived in a house for over 40 years and was elderly, they had no mortgage, and my questions started off with that assumption. Fortunately, they quickly corrected me, but if they hadn't my resolution to their problem may have been totally wrong.

As indicated in the last example, all is not necessarily lost if you get your questioning wrong – but why risk it in the first place?

Your questioning style is just as applicable when speaking to a potential investor as there is so much information that would help you meet their needs. Are they looking for a joint venture partnership? If you are looking for a fixed-rate loan, how much have they got to offer, at what rate and over how long? (A multiple question there but it does make it easier to write!) Have they been an investor for long? Have they had an investment go wrong? How did they deal with that? You get the picture, I am sure.

Questioning is an area we can all improve on after a conversation and reflecting on 'who said what, when, why and how!' But more of that in the Reflect stage later.

TIP 7: START OFF GENTLY

If you are attending a viewing with a seller then have a loose system around which you will ask the questions.

One system would be:

- Build rapport and find common ground.
- Ask questions about the house – structure, extensions, location etc.
- Ask questions about the reasons for sale.
- Ask questions about their personal financial situation if it is an integral part of the reason for the sale.

I suggest this order because it builds from non-emotive, easy-to-answer questions up to the more personal and intimate areas that they may find difficult to answer. By that stage though, you will have them talking freely and it is easier for you to move naturally into a more contentious area.

I suggest it is a loose system because you should avoid being dogmatic in your approach and, through your active listening, go with the flow of the conversation and respond accordingly.

By having a system, it means you feel more confident. If the conversation dries up, you have something to fall back on, or, if the seller keeps avoiding the questions or trying to distract you, then you know you can come back to them at the appropriate time.

TIP 8: BE PREPARED TO ASK DIFFICULT QUESTIONS

As I suggested in the last tip, you are going to have to ask what might be perceived as difficult or intimate questions.

Remember: you cannot solve any issue unless you fully understand what the issue is from both sides – and the only way to do that is by having ALL the information.

I see posts on social media daily where people are asking for advice about completing deals, when it becomes obvious immediately that they are looking at the problem from their position only. They do not have enough information to make an informed decision about the correct strategy, needs of the seller or the best win-win scenario.

So be prepared to ask those questions that elicit all the information. If there are financial issues, then you will need to be exploring that side of the reason for the sale.

One way to preface the questions is to set the tone of the conversation by saying something such as, "In order for me to fully understand the situation and be able to come up with a solution that suits all sides, then I may need to ask you some questions which may feel a bit personal. Is that ok?"

It takes a strong person to say, "No," to another person, so the likelihood is that they will say, "Yes," and they have now given permission for you go ahead. You can remind them of this later if they are still reluctant to answer. I understand that there is a point that you may wish to not push them past, but do not start to resolve the issue until you feel satisfied that you have all the information.

Why? Because the real reasons will always come out days, weeks or months down the line after you have spent valuable time, energy and possibly money on a deal that may not go through. Get the information from the start.

TIP 9: VIEWING SHEET AND PICTURES

As discussed in the preparation stage, you should have your viewing sheet with you to complete – either to use for your own due diligence and research (e.g. pricing up what needs to be done) or to pass on the lead to someone else.

Early in the conversation, you should make a judgement call when to use it – if at all. Remember, we stated that some deals are not worth doing, so don't waste time unless it is definitely one you will pass to someone else.

Consider taking pictures with your mobile phone/camera, although it is very important to ask for the permission of the seller or the accompanying viewer first. This will help you with recalling all the details later, especially if you have done several viewings in one day.

Using the viewing sheet also helps makes you look professional and organised which assists in building trust when it comes to negotiating the actual deal.

Also, if the deal is not accepted, then you can file the paperwork away in your 'follow-up' system and retrieve it a month later to see if they have become more motivated to do a deal.

CHAPTER SEVEN

EVOLVE

The premise behind this stage of the model is making sure that:

- You approach the situation with an open mind,
- Although you have a plan, you need to be flexible,
- You don't adopt a position before finding out all the issues, as things are often not what they seem to be.

In other words, actively listen to the responses to your questions, see the situation from their point of view and start to formulate your plans around the information given rather than your assumptions, perceptions or preconceived ideas.

A simple example is you might attend the viewing thinking about buying the property but after speaking to the seller you realise that that is not viable as they are in negative equity (they owe more on the mortgage than the property is worth). You therefore need to explore other strategies to acquire the property with them. The situation has evolved from the one you thought you were facing.

Again, many of the coachees I have spoken to over the years go to viewings, investment meetings and situations with a preconceived plan and have little or no information about the seller, their needs or the circumstances of the sale.

TIP 1: FORGET A POSITION – FIND THE ISSUE

What do I mean by position versus issue?

People tend to adopt a position and then work from it. For example, you enter the discussion thinking that you want to pay a certain price for a property. The seller's position is they want a certain price too and it is unlikely to be the same price as yours. You should then work towards a price that suits both sides.

However, the danger is that the more you try to justify your position (your price), the more the other person may become entrenched in their position (their price). Compromise therefore becomes more difficult.

A further complication is that if you take an extreme position and make small movements towards the other person's position, then it makes for a protracted and drawn-out negotiation.

This may draw you in to the hard-bargaining position versus the soft-bargaining position. Someone is going to lose – thereby creating a lose-win scenario.

Ethically, and also for long-term relationship building with estate agents and for your profile, it is much more advantageous to create that sometimes elusive win-win scenario.

Find out what the issue is for all sides and come up with a solution to that. You will be surprised how often the issue is not the price!

TIP 2: WHAT'S DRIVING THEM?

Part of understanding the issues involved goes back to the Engage and Explore stages of understanding what makes people 'tick'. People are emotional creatures and we buy and sell on emotion.

Find out what is important to them.

For some sellers it will be that they like you, feel they can trust you and want to do business with you.

For some estate agents, it will be that you are honest, trustworthy and they know that if you say you will buy then you will make that process easy for them.

For some investors, it is that you are not only giving them a great rate of return on their money, but also you will keep them informed on a weekly/monthly basis of the progress of the development.

Different personality types will respond to different stimuli – so find out what ticks their checklist.

When I am buying a car, a good salesperson knows not to talk to me about power of the engine, 0 to 60 speed, or other specifications. I am not interested. Talk to me about reliability, comfort and economy and I'm all ears. (Oh, and the colour!)

As soon as you make assumptions about what you think they want, you'll end up disappointed.

So, the conversations evolve as you start to learn what is driving them in this situation and you can then respond accordingly.

TIP 3: WHO IS THE DECISION MAKER?

Make sure you are dealing with the decision maker.

This is especially true if the property is being sold because of a separation/divorce – then whose name is on the mortgage? If both parties are title owners, then you now know you must understand the issues of two people. Unfortunately for you, those issues might be diametrically opposed! Not a quick negotiation.

If the property is a probate sale, has everything been signed off in respect of the will or the deceased estate planning? What else needs to happen with the will before a deal can be struck? How many persons are involved in the estate, or can the appointed executors sign off on the deal? Our probate purchase took eight months to get over the line.

If chatting to an investor, is it just their money or will they have to run the proposal through their life/business partner before they can commit to investing? They will not always tell you this up-front, so it is worth exploring. If it is the case, your conversation has evolved to finding out what the third party may want/need too.

TIP 4: STAY IN CONTROL

It is important to stay in control of the conversation and we have helped you start doing that in the future by introducing you to the PER model and the Planning, Prepare and Practising phase.

By having structure, you can make sure you keep on track with the reason for the meeting and there is less chance of being ambushed by something you have not thought of.

Be flexible and respond to the conversation as it evolves, but make sure this is taking you in the direction you need to go in order to secure a deal at some point in the future.

Prevent the seller or investor distracting you from the purpose of the meeting by re-directing the conversation to where you want it to go. I have spent many conversations going around in circles with individuals who don't want to get to the centre of the issues involved. You are helping some people face up to the realities of their situation and that can be difficult for them.

Imagine the emotions that a divorcing seller is going through – having to acknowledge that they are not only losing a relationship, but also all the material things that go with it (including the house).

Your role is to manage the situation before you and help to find a solution to their problem as empathically as possible.

And you thought it was just about buying houses!!

TIP 5: CUT IT SHORT

If appropriate, be prepared to cut the conversation short in a professional and appropriate way.

Following on from the above scenario – if their emotions get the better of them, and you think it appropriate, either take a break from the conversation or agree to meet again in the future at an agreed time and date. It's not a problem to say, "I can see you're upset, so it might be more appropriate for us to continue this discussion at another time. You can collect your thoughts and we'll be able to carry on where we've left it today."

If the new information they are giving starts to overwhelm you – either because you need to re-examine the figures or think through the most appropriate strategy to create that win-win deal – don't feel pushed in to making decisions. Explain exactly that: based on the new information you feel it best to go away and carry out some further research so that you can come with the best solution to suit all the parties.

If you are with an investor and they're pushing to invest with you almost immediately, you might want to place the onus on them to go away and think about it more. They can make sure they are comfortable with going forward and they may also think of new questions to ask that they haven't currently thought of. Entering into investment agreements – even fixed loan arrangements – needs to be thought through carefully and I would be cautious of dealing with someone who is too eager. It might indicate lack of due diligence on their part and problems for you in the future.

In the worst-case scenario: as the conversation evolves, it may become evident that even with the best-laid plans and the greatest skillset in the world, there are times when it is just not worth doing the deal – withdraw.

TIP 6: RECOGNISE YOUR KNOWLEDGE GAPS

As the situation or identified issue evolves and new information comes to light, you might become aware that there are gaps in your knowledge of property strategies, experience and the legalities of some of the issues you are presented with.

Do not be afraid of this – nobody knows everything there is to know about all the new regulations, laws, strategies and problems that are developing every day.

Do not bluff your way through. If the circumstances have changed based on what the seller, estate agent or investor have now told you, acknowledge that.

Suggest to them that, "I need to take some time to digest the new information and in order for me to come up with a solution that meets your interests, then I'd like to come back to you very soon with an answer. Is that ok by you?"

Does this show weakness or lack of professionalism on your part? I don't think so if you position it in the right way – namely, in order to provide a better service/outcome or conclusion for them.

TIP 7: GO WITH YOUR GUT INSTINCT

I am often asked whether you should go with your gut instinct in respect of deals and especially when considering joint venture partnerships.

I believe there two main reasons for listening to your instincts and going with them:

- If you ignore your intuition and go with the investor/investment and the deal goes wrong, it is so much harder to forgive yourself and move on. Even if your due diligence reveals no issues, there will still be that little voice in your head that says, "I knew I shouldn't have done it. I could feel something wasn't quite right at the time." Much harder to move on with little voices!

- Secondly, I sincerely believe that your gut instinct is a result of all the messages being picked up by your sub-conscious, giving you warning signals. You are picking up subtle clues and nuances the other person is inadvertently sending which your brain is processing and telling you, "No."

So, based on this, go with your instinct and move on right away. There is always another deal to be done or an investor to work with.

PHASE THREE

REAL ESTATE
AGENT

CHAPTER EIGHT

RESOLVE

In many instances, the Evolve stage will naturally move into the Resolve stage and that is how it should be in a flexible, natural conversation.

There is an important distinction to be made here though in that Resolve relates to THIS conversation, not necessarily the whole issue being addressed. It goes back to the earlier stages of planning and preparation for this conversation. Remember we should ask, "What is a realistic outcome for the conversation or meeting?"

So, Resolve in this instance refers to the conclusion of the conversation and the next steps that one or both parties will take following on from the decisions or actions agreed. This can range from thanking the person and agreeing there is no future in the relationship through to what the next steps will be for setting up a deal or investment contract/partnership.

Under these tips though, I have also included the next steps that you might consider taking.

TIP 1: SET CLEAR ACTIONS

It is important that if there are actions to be taken that you set clear, specific steps and deadlines outlining who does what, and by when.

Check each other's understanding of these steps and what they mean.

Does, "I'll contact the solicitor this week" mean, "I'll contact the solicitor and just leave a message," or does it mean, "I will contact the solicitor and get a response by Friday of this week?"

If appropriate, fill out a formal action plan or schedule of who does what actions and next steps.

TIP 2: NDAs and HEADS OF TERMS AGREEMENT

If you are dealing with a seller direct, then if appropriate, consider completing a Non-Disclosure Agreement. This is a contract through which the parties agree not to disclose information covered by the agreement. This would typically include: agreed prices, property details and personal details of the parties involved. An NDA creates a confidential relationship between the parties, typically to protect any type of confidential information.

Or, if appropriate, consider creating a Heads of Terms agreement – particularly in relation to purchase lease options and lease options. A HOT is a summary proposal of the commercial terms that both the parties would like the lease document to include such as each other's details, the property details, the length of the lease option, the option fee, any monthly fee and special conditions.

The Heads of Terms are not legally enforceable, and you should not rely on them for contractual protection. A deal is only truly agreed once both parties have signed formal documents and the transaction is completed. However, they are useful for psychologically tying the other party to the deal and giving to your respective solicitors to draw up the agreement.

Similarly, when dealing with a potential investor, it might be useful to draw up an agreement with just the basic outlines of your discussion and agreement, if one has been made, so that it can be referred to when formulating a formal contract.

TIP 3: GET USED TO HEARING "NO!"

It is suggested in property circles that you should aim for a "NO" when making offers for properties you are interested in acquiring. The reasoning is that if the person agrees to your first offer, then basically you have offered TOO much.

Therefore, it helps if you get used to hearing, "No" when your first offer is made. In fact, I have heard one individual state, "Never mind the seller, if YOU are not embarrassed by the offer, then you have offered too much."

Although I subscribe to the view that you are in this business to make money (and most money is often made at the point of purchase), I do firmly believe in making below-market offers which are ethically sound as well as reflecting your due diligence around comparables and other similar property prices. How far below market value you are prepared to go will be dictated by your own ethics, values and whether you genuinely believe in creating win-win scenarios for all the parties.

Some people I believe are taking the below-market-value mantra to new levels though. As a result, I am seeing agents and sellers becoming frustrated with what they believe are timewasters putting in absurdly low offers – some at 50 and 60% below market value. My view is that this is not the way to build a professional, long-term relationship, particularly with agents who you should be encouraging to bring you new leads in the future.

TIP 4: "NO" DOESN'T MEAN NO. IT MEANS "NO, NOT NOW."

Any offer that you make should reflect your due diligence and what the figures indicate your investment is for this property. You should know up to what price you are prepared to pay (and that could sometimes be the asking price on a great investment!)

Do not become a motivated buyer and go above your researched price unless you have new information (such as you now realise that that large rear garden has room to build another property on it). Even then, manage your emotions and resolve this discussion by agreeing to get back to them because you want to go away and conduct more research on the cost of building a property on that land.

If you show you are too eager, then they will pick up on it. I have been guilty of this in the past and the seller realises their property is worth more than they are currently asking and shifts their position accordingly.

Once you have conducted your further research, you can plan another conversation based around that research and get back to them to recommence the conversation.

Should they still say, "No," then tell them the offer will stay 'on the table' and place it in your system to follow up in a few weeks' time to see if their stance has changed. If so, great do the deal. If not, follow up again in a further few weeks.

One of my best deals was on the third follow-up call after two previous flat refusals to accept my offer.

TIP 5: PROMISES, PROMISES.

Do not fall into the trap of making false promises or give false hope to make yourself feel more comfortable.

Be conscious of using phrases like, "I'm sure we can work something out," or "I'm sure we can do that," or "No problem, leave it with me. I'm sure we can come to some arrangement." They seem like insignificant phrases often thrown into the conversation, but people who are in a desperate situation selling their house will possibly pick up on these as concrete assertions. Avoid them.

All these phrases are often made to make US feel better because we don't want to disappoint the other person and say, "No."

You are running a professional property business – it's not a hobby. Do your research and due diligence and the figures do not lie. If it is doable – great. If it's not, say so.

TIP 6: KEEP A SYSTEM FOR CONTACTS

Whilst being aware of your General Data Protection Regulation 2018 (GDPR) responsibilities in the UK and European Union, think about keeping a system of the contacts you have made and under what circumstances.

As stated above, if a deal is not made then you should keep it in your follow-up system anyway. However, what about potential investors who might want to work with you?

Certainly, in my early days of investing, I failed to set up a system and regretted it. Once you start getting out there – attending networking meetings, shows, and events letting people know that you are investing in property and starting to build a reputation for delivering on deals or projects – people will want to invest with you. As a result, you will have more and more important conversations with others. You can then lose track of who's who and what they want.

It does not have to be complicated – a simple spreadsheet will suffice at first.

Once you have met the potential investor, then record a few details such as: name, contact details, type of investment they are interested in (fixed loan or JV partnership). If fixed rate, what rate over how long? What type of development or properties are they are interested in? How much funding do they have available? How quickly can they access those funds? Are they a high-net-worth individual or a sophisticated investor? (See UK Financial Conduct Authority rules).

This spreadsheet becomes useful as you can refer to it when you find a deal and may be looking for investment funds and need to move quickly.

CHAPTER NINE

REFLECT

You now come to one of the most important stages of the model and certainly one of the hardest to master – Reflecting on the conversation and how to improve for the future.

Thinking about how the logistics went is a relatively straightforward part. Questions such as: was the location suitable, did I leave long enough to cover everything, was the time of day suitable, did I leave time to travel? are all easy to answer and require no deep thought.

My experience after over 40 years of debriefing incidents and individuals is that they tend to look at the situation from an overall perspective and rarely drill down deeper than a superficial, 'It went ok.'

Being a dedicated, honest and balanced reflective practitioner takes time, effort and sometimes painful growth. However, once mastered, it will help you through all aspects of your life, not just important conversations.

For this reflective stage, I am really focusing on YOUR part in the conversation. Why? Because that is the part you have 100 per cent control over. You cannot control what they said or did, albeit as the PER model shows, you can start to influence it.

Knowing how to reflect on the conversation covers all conversations and it doesn't matter if it was with an estate agent, seller or investor. The principles are the same.

TIP 1: ASK YOURSELF THE RIGHT QUESTIONS

Like the planning and preparation stage, make a list of useful questions that you need to ask yourself.

It is said in personal development circles that the quality of a person's life is relative to the quality of the questions a person is willing to ask themselves.

I would go further and say that quality is dependent on, "the quality of the questions you ask and the quality of the answers you give."

Being honest and balanced in your answers can be the painful part.

Some I could think of are:

- What went well?
- What could be improved?
- What would I not do next time?
- Was my Planning complete?
- Was my Preparation complete?
- What assumptions did I make?
- What questions could I have asked?
- What questions did I not need to ask?
- Did I answer each of their questions fully, competently, concisely?
- Did I manage my emotions?

The above is not a comprehensive list, but you can see that by starting to ask specific questions you can start to focus in on each aspect of the conversation.

Does this take a long time? At first it can, but as with any skill the more you practise the easier it becomes, and eventually you can focus in very quickly on the aspect you want to reflect upon.

TIP 2: HAVE A SYSTEM FOR RELECTION

For conversations, I like to go through the 4WH debrief system.

Who said what, when, why and how?

Work your way through the important parts of the conversation and ask yourself, "Who said what?"

Then, analysing your part, ask, "Was that the right time to say/question/comment what I did?" Should the question/comment have been made earlier or later at a more appropriate time?

Then ask, "Why did I say it? Did it need saying, or did I just say it to make myself feel better?" This "Why?" question is particularly important when reflecting on emotive or tense conversations as we tend to fill in the silences with inane or feel-good comments.

Then, the final crucial part, ask yourself, "How did I say it?" Remember that tone, body language, posture and voice level are all part of the reflection on "How" it was said.

If there was a 'trigger' point in the conversation – a point where it started to go wrong – it is very likely down to a comment or question being spoken at either the wrong time or in the wrong way.

Reflection is about learning from our mistakes and removing those 'trigger' points in the future.

However, in order to keep it balanced, remember going through the same system and looking for the positives.

"Who said what, when, why and how?" will also reveal what you did well and would want to keep for the future. A great answer to one of their questions should be celebrated and you should praise yourself.

TIP 3: SEEK FEEDBACK

Don't be afraid to seek feedback on any aspect of the conversation from a third party such as a coach or mentor whose experience and opinion you can trust and respect.

As you go through the process of the 4WH debrief, you can then relate that back to someone who you trust to give you evidenced and constructive feedback.

One of the potential shortcomings of self-reflecting can be the tendency to ask yourself great questions but then filter the answers through your own values, opinions, beliefs and cognitive biases. If you are not careful, you go into the "Yes but I did that because…" mode of self-reflection, and then try to justify what you said and how you said it.

Interestingly, it is easier to notice it in others when you challenge them over something they have said or done – and they will either blame someone/something else, make an excuse or (worse still) deny it even happened. (Fake news syndrome!)

So, if you can hear it in others, now be open and honest enough to be hearing it from yourself. As soon as you hear yourself say, "But..." be conscious that a self-justification may be coming.

Challenge yourself. Once you hear a self-justification, dig down deeper and ask, "Would I accept that answer from someone else…?" or "Ok, however, could I have done it differently?"

Hopefully you can now see that the use of a coach or mentor can be incredibly powerful.

It cuts out the danger of not being completely honest and balanced in your reflection, as they can listen and then help you by delving deeper into what occurred and how it could be done differently next time. Their questioning of your answers will help bring clarity and focus to what went on and what changes in phrasing will help you in the future.

TIP 4: DECISIONS CAN BE CHANGED

During this reflect stage, also think about any decisions you may have made in the conversation.

Are they the right ones?

Did you get carried away in the moment and now you've had the time and space to reflect about the conversation, should you change those decisions?

Has your further due diligence and research, based on what was said, turned up a complication that you were not aware of?

If so, better to withdraw or renegotiate the deal now rather than being afraid to say, "No," and potentially feel embarrassed about it.

You are making important and life-changing decisions that must be right.

Just as you should get accustomed to hearing, "No" from sellers and estate agents then you should get used to hearing yourself say, "No" too.

CHAPTER TEN

REFINE

I was once facilitating a role-playing session with an individual who, although they had performed reasonably well during the de-brief of the incident, several areas were identified for them to develop and improve. At the time they did not take the feedback too well and became defensive, justifying their actions.

However, to their credit, they came back into the group the next day and started by saying in a forthright way, "I spent last night thinking about my session yesterday and I would only change three things."

As a facilitator, this was music to my ears. I responded by genuinely praising them for taking the time to self-reflect and adding, "If you go through your career just changing one thing to improve after each incident, never mind three, then you will make an excellent officer!"

Many people go through life not reflecting honestly and as a result they do not improve or change. They confuse 20 years of doing the same thing as 20 years' experience when, in fact, experience comes from trying, changing adapting and growing.

Therefore, being open to Refining your actions is crucial to your development, as well as knowing what to change, and why you are changing it.

TIP 1: DO I NEED TO CHANGE?

There is sometimes a tendency to change things because we feel we ought to. Do not make changes for change's sake – in effect, "Don't fix it if it isn't broken!"

I accept there are times when we want to try out something new and if that is the reason, then go with it. Basically, if you make a change, make sure you understand the reason for doing so.

However, if you are trying something new, check you can test and measure the outcomes against what you currently do.

Unless you test and measure, then you cannot compare like with like and make improvements needed.

Be aware of your cognitive filters and biases telling you it went ok but if you did something well and it worked – keep it.

TIP 2: MARGINAL GAINS

It is important to realise that you do not necessarily have to make wholesale changes to your style, questioning technique, language or approach.

Sometimes the changes are very subtle, but the outcome can be huge.

I was recently coaching an individual who stated that they had met a potential investor and she was disappointed that they had asked for a high interest rate on the proposed fixed-term private loan they were looking to enter in to. He had mentioned 10% whereas she was hoping he would say 6%.

I asked her to tell me what she had specifically said to him. She replied, "I asked him what his ideal rate would be." I discussed with her the ramifications of using the word 'ideal" and what it evokes in the mind. She agreed "ideal" can mean existing only in your imagination; it's desirable or even perfect.

I then posed the question to her, "What would have been the difference if you had asked him, 'What would be a reasonable rate for you?'" That potentially invokes a totally different mindset in the investor. He is now thinking REASONABLE rather than IDEAL.

I have no idea if the outcome would have been different – however, why risk the same thing happening in the future when the changing of one word has the potential to influence someone's decision.

TIP 3: FURTHER EVIDENCE

Like the question, 'Do I need to change it?" above, sometimes during self-reflection we need to ask ourselves whether what happened was potentially a 'one- off' occurrence, or possibly a coincidence.

If we feel it is appropriate, then in these circumstances we should note what happened or what was said and then include in our planning for future similar conversations to watch out for the outcome of that question or comment that we made.

If, on the second occasion a similar result occurs, then we have confirmation of our original thoughts and we can amend our language, question or comment accordingly.

TIP 4: BACK TO CONSCIOUSLY COMPETENT

Familiarise yourself with the Conscious Competence model of learning and recognise where you are in it for different aspects of your property experience.

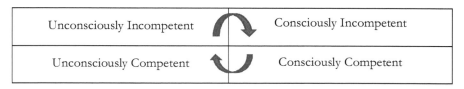

Unconsciously Incompetent	Consciously Incompetent
Unconsciously Competent	Consciously Competent

We move through the different levels as we take on and learn a new skill as follows:

Unconsciously Incompetent >>> Consciously Incompetent >>> Consciously Competent >>> Unconsciously Competent.

Once we get to where we believe we are Unconsciously Competent – in other words we do not have to think about the skill as we naturally do it – there is danger we become complacent and start to take things for granted.

A good example might be rapport building in the Engage stage.

Imagine that we believe we get so good at it that we feel that we can naturally walk into any environment, meet and greet people, build trust quickly and have them hanging on our every word.

This might well be the case for some of the time.

However, we then start to 'wing it' or get overconfident which could result in us making assumptions, not actively listening and forgetting the basics of good open questions, silence and positive body language.

We now need to refine what we are doing and go back into the Consciously Competent phase of the model which some people don't like to do as it feels as if they are going backwards.

We are all constantly learning so don't be too proud to move past thinking, 'I know that,' and constantly re-checking in with yourself.

CHAPTER ELEVEN

SUMMARY

AND FINAL TIPS!

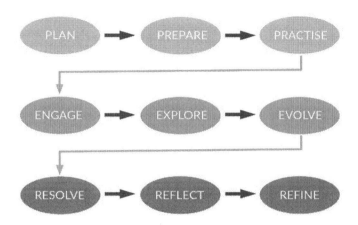

Well, that's the whole model covered as well as the tips and strategies to help you apply it over the coming months and years.

You might also like to think about how it could help you with other crucial conversations you need to have in other areas of your life such as the workplace, relationships and leisure pursuits!

An advantage of having a structured approach to your conversations is that you know where you are in the model and can focus on the areas that you need to develop. Until you become unconsciously competent, you can use the whole model going through each phase in turn.

However, as your confidence and experience grow, you can decide which parts to use for different types of conversations and scenarios or how deep you go with each part, making sure, of course, that you do not slip into complacency.

Because this model has set stages, you can apply parts of it or all of it to each of your conversations. You will know where you are in the process and it makes the process of reflect and refine, as you go along, much easier.

Your confidence and professionalism will increase significantly the more you apply it and you will see the improved results as you connect with more estate/letting agents and potential investors. Following on from those well-established connections you will agree more deals, create better deals and enter into more joint venture partnerships.

FINAL TIPS

It is not a race – follow your own path to building your property wealth.

Do not compare yourself with others – we all start with different resources (including time and money) and skills.

Avoid get-rich-quick schemes – a sustainable property business takes hard work and commitment.

Invest in quality specialist property education.

Obtain the services of a knowledgeable coach and mentor (more than one for different areas of your business.)

Reward yourself after each success.

But none of it matters if you do not get out there and **TAKE ACTION**.

ADDENDUM

Questions You Might Ask

A Vendor:

Remember that for you to help them in the best way you can, and create a deal which satisfies both your needs, some questions may seem personal regarding their situation.

- How can I help you?
- How long have you lived in the property?
- Why do you feel the need to sell?
- How much interest has there been in the property? (If it has been on the market).
- Have you had any offers? – If yes, what were they and why did you turn them down?
- What do you really want?
- What would be the best outcome for you?
- How is this affecting you financially, emotionally or personally? (Say "Thank you for being open with me," and continue with further short prompts like, "and," "anything else?" and "Is that everything?"
- How is this affecting those around you?
- What do you intend doing with the money once the deal is complete?
- What would that mean to you / how would it help you?
- What are you looking for from me?
- Do you have a time scale?
- Is there anyone else linked to the deal who has an interest? (Relevant when dealing with divorces, multiple owners, companies etc.)
- Do you have a mortgage on the property? If yes, how much is outstanding on the mortgage?

- How much a month is the mortgage repayment?
- How much time is left to go on the mortgage?
- Are there any other debts linked to the property?
- Do you have any other financial considerations regarding this sale?
- Are there any structural / maintenance issues with the property?
- Have similar properties in the road had extensions/planning approvals or been refused planning?
- Is there access to the garden other than the front drive?
- Are there any covenants or restrictions on the properties?
- Have any alterations or building work been carried out and when was it done?
- If any alterations or building work have been carried out, does it have the appropriate permissions, licences, consents, planning, certificates?
- Is the property in a conservation area or does it have planning restrictions?

An Estate Agent:

- Do you have any properties that you are finding it difficult to sell?
- Do you have any properties that are not mortgageable?
- Do you know any sellers who are needing to sell quickly for cash?
- Do you have any properties that are embarrassing to show people round?
- Do you have any properties that have fallen through several times?
- Do you have any properties that are refurbishment/conversion projects?
- Do you have any properties that are being sold by a retiring landlord?
- Do you have any properties that, with a change of use, would be more desirable?

A Potential Investor:

- Have you invested in property before? If so, in what way? How did that work out?

- Are you looking for a fixed loan or potential Joint Venture (JV)?

If Fixed Loan:

- What rate of interest would you be looking for? For how long? Interest payments rolled up to the end or paid monthly?
- If payment of capital was delayed, how would this affect you?
- What security do you need, if any?
- Do you have a solicitor to draw up a contract or could we use mine?
- What percentage of your savings are you investing? (This is based around my own values/beliefs as I would not want someone to invest all their life savings with me.)
- If they're using joint savings, are other interested parties aware? (e.g. their life partner, business partner)
- Will you be declaring this loan to any interested lender?

If Joint Venture:

Full joint ventures should not be entered into lightly as you have the potential to lose not only your potential profits, but if things go wrong there could be legal fees incurred as well as the emotional energy wasted and time lost. I would therefore expect them to ask me as many questions as I ask them. I need to know that they fully understand the legal and moral obligations that a joint venture 50/50 deal entails.

- What joint ventures have you done in the past?
- Who have you done them with?
- How are the legal arrangements set up?
- Have you had a joint venture go wrong? If so, how did you handle it?
- What is our exit strategy should it go wrong?
- What happens if one of the parties becomes incapacitated or – in a worst-case scenario – dies?
- Can I see your credit file?
- What life insurance do you have?
- What are the tax implications for a joint venture?

What They Might Ask You

The questions you get asked will depend on the person you are dealing with, but this gives you a broad idea of what might be asked.

Vendor:

- Can you guarantee that you will buy my property?
- What are you going to do with the property?
- If I accept your offer how long will it take to complete the deal?
- Will you pay my legal fees / expenses?
- If I come direct to you, what about the estate agent / auction house?
- Will we sign an agreement if I accept your offer?
- If we sign an agreement, is there a cooling-off period?
- Will you give me market value?
- Why is your offer so low?

Investor:

- What previous property experience do you have?
- How many properties do you own / control?
- What types of properties do you have?
- How long have you been dealing in property?
- Have you done a deal like this before?
- Can you provide any references?
- Do you have any other financial interests / businesses?
- How quickly can you move?
- Who is your solicitor / broker?
- Can I be involved in the development process?
- Have you ever had a County Court Judgement (CCJ) against you?
- Have you ever been declared bankrupt? What were the circumstances?

Estate Agent:

- Have you bought other properties in the area?

- Why have you chosen this area?
- How quickly can you move?
- Can you provide proof of funds?
- Who is your solicitor / broker?
- Do you have a mortgage decision in principle?
- What are you intending to do with the property? – if they are a local independent agent they may object to an HMO / flats in their town.
- Are you a cash buyer?

Potential Investor:

See the above questions you might ask them, and expect to also have them asked by the other party. I would expect them to ask me as many questions as I ask them. I need to know that they fully understand the legal and moral obligations that a joint venture 50/50 deal entails.

You need to have the answers to their questions!!

About the Property

As well as questions about the physical structure of the property you might ask or note:

- How long have you owned / held the property?
- Have any previous sales fallen through? If so, why?
- What previous offers have you had?
- Are there any maintenance issues you are aware of?
- How old is the boiler? Is there a warranty on it? What size is it?
- Do you have the Gas Safety Certificate (if applicable).
- How old are the electrics? (Be wary of old-school landlords who maintain the properties themselves. They are unregistered electricians/gas fitters and often their work needs making safe!!)
- Do you have the Electrical Certificate (if applicable).
- How old is the central heating system?
- How big is the plot size / garden? (Is there potential to add value?)
- Has there been a planning application submitted previously that has

been granted/lapsed or refused?

- Have similar properties in the road had extensions/planning approvals or been refused planning?
- Is there access to the garden other than the front drive?
- Are there any covenants or restrictions on the property?
- Have any alterations or building work been carried out and when was it done?
- If any alterations or building work have been carried out, does it have the appropriate permissions, licences, consents, planning, certificates, etc.
- Is the area the house is in a conservation area or does it have planning restrictions?
- If leasehold, what is the length of the lease, service charges, lease terms and conditions?
- Have there been any issues with neighbours?
- What are the local services like? (Transport, schools, hospitals, doctors, shops, pubs, etc.)
- What are the local council planning office plans for the area?
- Has a strategic planning policy been published for the area?
- Are there any issues regarding flooding?
- Are there any issues with parking – do you need a resident's permit?
- Are there seasonal considerations with parking, (e.g, in a popular holiday location?)
- What is the commuting potential / issues?
- Are there any hostels/vulnerable housing properties nearby?

Financials:

- Is the property unencumbered (no mortgage / bond)?
- What is the current outstanding mortgage / bond?
- Are they currently able to get a mortgage?
- Are there any other outstanding loans against them and / or the property?
- What other businesses do they have a financial interest in?

- Who are the lenders?
- Does anyone else have a first charge (or second charge etc.) against the property?
- Is there an RX1 linked to the property?
- Are you be prepared to sign a Letter of Authority to enable me to speak to the lender(s)?
- In respect of the valuations given are they: the vendor's own figures; the estate agent's; RICS (Royal Institute of Surveyors)?
- Do they know how much other similar properties in the area have recently sold for?
- Do they have any other outstanding loans, expenses, or financials that will have a bearing on the deal?
- Do they require the money from the deal for a specific reason?
- What are they going to do with the money from the deal?
- Have they ever been declared bankrupt?
- Do they have any CCJ's against them?
- Are they in the process of being repossessed?
- What stage of the repossession process are they – have they been to court?
- Can I see the documentation from the lenders in respect of the repossession?

Due Diligence – Desktop Research

When conducting your due diligence the following links and sites are a useful place to start;

General Area Research:

- Google maps
- Data Observatory
- Facebook
- Checkmystreet – https://www.checkmystreet.co.uk/
- Streetcheck – https://www.streetcheck.co.uk/

Checking Out the Seller:

- Contact details – Name and telephone number
- ID and proof of address
- Title and ownership (one or several people)
- Land Registry – check owner of property and titles
- Bankruptcy / Insolvency Register
- https://www.gov.uk/government/organisations/land-registry
- https://www.gov.uk/search-bankruptcy-insolvency-register

Checking Out the Property:

- Property type
- Property structure
- Internal layout – number of bedrooms / bathrooms / reception rooms
- External – garage, gardens, shed
- Take pictures – with permission

To Help Determine the Property Market Value

Comparables:

- Rightmove
- Zoopla
- Mouseprice
- On the Market
- https://www.rightmove.co.uk/house-prices.html
- https://www.zoopla.co.uk/house-prices/
- https://www.mouseprice.com/
- https://www.onthemarket.com/sold-prices/

Checking Out Valuations for a Remortgage of a Property:

Extra trackers working on Rightmove through Google Chrome

- HomeBuyer-beta: https://chrome.google.com/webstore/detail/home-buyer-beta/kdmfpdcbfbfgidmchkdakmoihliofnme

- Property Tracker add-on for Chrome: https://chrome.google.com/webstore/detail/property-tracker/abgkpdjomdmemeefdefalbeogkmlmand

To check the street, neighbourhood and exterior of property:

- https://mapstreetview.com/
- www.streetcheck.co.uk
- www.dataobservatory.co.uk
- www.googleearth.com

Call estate agents in the area posing as a buyer or seller.

To check out what the owner paid and when:

- https://www.zoopla.co.uk/house-prices/
- https://nethouseprices.com/
- https://www.nationwide.co.uk/about/house-price-index/house-price-calculator

Owners own valuation: how and when was it done?

Consider a RICS valuation (only when you want to buy)

https://www.hometrack.com/uk/

https://propertydata.co.uk/ (less practical than hometrack, more affordable, nice market trends for sale and rent)

Land:

- Value if planning permission gained.
- Key features: size, location, type of land (arable, brownfield, garden), planning permission and for what purpose (still valid).
- Work possible price backwards from Gross Development Value (GDV).
- Maximum purchase price = GDV - 20%-25% profit investor - sourcing fee (when applicable) - build & finance costs.
- Ideally on land, sign a PLO to get planning and sell with an extra benefit.

- Way of sourcing and having a gross estimate of construction costs:
- Go on council portal and look at people that have their planning submission either declined or withdrawn.
- Compare similar projects for building costs preliminary evaluation.

Commercial Property:

- Rental income, profitability (EBITDA) for hotels.
- Yield/multiplier that depends on location and type of business.
- Check with local commercial agent, commercial surveyor (RICS) (often at commercial agents) and commercial broker to use the appropriate yield.

Rental Value & Demand:

- Check websites Rightmove, Zoopla, Hometrack, Propertydata, Spareroom for comparables.
- Call Letting agents (posing as prospective tenant).

Possible added value:

- Planning for land.
- Structural repair.
- Renovate.
- Extend.
- New Build.
- Subdivide.
- Change use (HMO, SA, new type of tenants, Commercial to Residential).
- Cost of work to add value, including 10% to 20% contingencies.
- Possibility of little or no money left in with momentum finance.

Deal Analysis:

- Use spreadsheets for different types of properties and include key financials, and compare several exit strategies.
- Cashflow & Return on Investment.
- Refurbishment costs.

- Planner/Architect's fees.
- Specialist's fees – Environmental survey, Ecological, Flood Risk etc.
- Planning Costs.
- Legal fees.
- Stamp Duty.

Additional Due Diligence for a House of Multiple Occupancy:

- Article 4 Restrictions in place?
- Building Regulations.
- Planning Requirements.
- License Requirements.
- Covenants on the use of the property (often single-let only).
- Local area considerations: parking, bike space, bin storage, noise.

Property Viewing Checklist

DATE VIEWED: BY WHOM:	
Property Address:	
Reason For Sale:	
Type of Property:	
Structure / Year Built:	
Freehold / Leasehold:	
Outbuildings	
Gardens	

EXTERNAL

Chimney	
Roof	
Gutters	
Drainage	
Windows	
Doors	
Other	

GARDENS

Front	
Rear	
Side	
Hedges	
Fencing	
Driveway	
Gates	
Access	
Other	

OUTBUILDINGS

Garage	
Shed	
Summer House	
Greenhouse	
Workshop	
Office	
Other	

INTERNAL

Porch	Entrance Hall
Reception Room 1	Reception Room 2
Reception Room 3	Kitchen
Utility Room	Downstairs Cloakroom / WC
Stairs / Landing	Bedroom 1:
Bedroom 2:	Bedroom 3:
Bedroom 4:	Bathroom:
Attic / Cellar	Conservatory
Double Glazing	Central Heating

OTHER NOTES

Printed in Poland
by Amazon Fulfillment
Poland Sp. z o.o., Wrocław

60725160R00070